"*Career Switch* is a brilliant coach, a best friend, and a been-there-done-that guide to ditching your career demons and finding work you truly care about. As author Melani Ward reminds us, "Career satisfaction is not a limited resource" -- though it can sometimes feel that way, particularly if you have started down one path and suddenly (or slowly and agonizingly) realize you are unfulfilled and in dire need of change. Ward provides the perfect mix of poignant personal anecdotes, client stories and coaching exercises to help you diffuse your fears and figure out what's next, all through the lens of her thought-provoking letter-writing approach. Ward's wisdom and hard-won career switches shine through every page. In fact, the publication of this very book is evidence that her dream-tending strategy works, just as it can for you."
Jenny Blake, author of *Life After College*

"This is like no journal book I've ever seen. This is not about just writing your dreams down and then crossing your fingers in hopes they come true. It's not about just learning who you are in theory. It's about acting on behalf of your curiosities, desires and hopes right now so that you can learn about who you are in practice…information you'll need if you ever hope to make a living doing work you love. Awesome!"
Sandy Grason, author of *Journalution*

"If doing work that makes you giddy with joy is what you have been searching for, then you're going to love love love this book. Melani is a potent combo of loving teacher, saucy task-master and cool best friend. This book will set fire to your desire and guide you to take real action to DO the work you love. Enjoy!"
Jennifer Louden, author of *The Woman's Comfort Book* and *The Life Organizer*

Career Switch

Career Switch

How to Write & Play Your Way to Career Clarity

Melani Ward

Career Strategy Press

Boulder, Colorado

Career Strategy Press

Boulder, CO

Website: Careerswitch.org

All rights reserved.

ISBN: 1479300985

ISBN 13: 9781479300983

Library of Congress Control Number: 2012917172

CreateSpace Independent Publishing Platform

North Charleston, South Carolina

1. Career change 2. Careers 3. Career development 4. Self-actualization (Psychology)
5. Job satisfaction 6. Vocational guidance 7. Personality and occupation

Cover and interior design: Colleen Comer

Editor: Stephanie Gunning

Photo of Author: Amy Freeth Rice

To Mom, Dad, Topo, Chris and Dylan:
You make life good fun

Contents

Introduction

It's not too late to switch your career.

You can do work (or a job) you love. You can do work you care about.

You can.

You instantly felt the truth of it when I said it.

A tingle flew up your spine. Your heart beat faster.

Your heart beat faster because you know there's something you want to do for a living that you're *not* doing. Or at least you believe in the possibility that it exists: You could find that thing you love to do, that you care about more than anything if you searched for it.

When I said, "You can do *work you love*," perhaps you had a moment. You may have had a glimpse of yourself doing it (whatever it is for you), and it felt exhilarating.

Doing work we love, doing work that matters to us . . . is fair game for all of us. The reality of loving your work is not only reserved for a select few. Career satisfaction is not a limited resource. It therefore doesn't have to be something you consistently dream about, but don't experience. The question is: How do you search for it and find it?

Or maybe even more importantly, how do you search for it when it feels too complicated, or when you're scared you'll figure it out but won't be able to make it happen? How do you risk humiliation and failure when everyone in your life tells you you're mad, and when your inner critic tells you to get over it and move on?

Switching careers, starting your own business, or even re-entering the work force if you've been out of it for a while isn't easy; however it's a lot easier and far more fulfilling than sticking around in a job you hate or that leaves you emotionally empty. The thing is, most career changes fail—and not because they are a bad idea or because making a change was a bad decision. They fail because people give up on them too soon. They don't follow through or they decide to stay where they are.

Perhaps people give up on career switching because they lack belief in what they are doing or they don't have the network around to support them. Maybe it's just too difficult. But honestly, what could be more difficult than spending the day doing work that drains you, or that you don't care about, or that rattles you, or that makes you question yourself and your life on a day-to-day basis?

If you've been holding back from going after the work you truly care about, the question you have to face right now is: How will you become brave enough to go for that job or career which you've kept at arm's length, and then follow it through to the glorious end? Through my own personal journey of working with, and interviewing hundreds of people who have gone through career switches, I have concluded that one of the quickest ways to become brave is to get clarity on what you want.

Getting clarity sounds obvious and simplistic, and yet it is not. Sit down for cocktails or coffee with any of your friends and I suspect the majority of them will open up about something they're trying to get clarity on, whether it's their job, their intimate relationship, their preferred eating style, or where they should send their kids to school. They'll tell you how hard it is for them to gain clarity. We all want clarity and we talk about getting it, but in the end the word often winds up a floating bubble hovering over our heads as we move through life because we just don't know how to get it.

Clarity doesn't just happen to us. The clouds don't miraculously part merely because we say that's what we want. We have to *act* to get the clarity we seek. We have to do the work. We have to do the inner work *and* the outer work. When we do that, it gets pretty close to magic. That's why I have written an entire book on exactly how to achieve blissful clarity about the work you want to do.

Being Hell Bent

A lot of people might ask you, "What do you want to do when you retire?" As if that's when your life will truly be yours to live as spectacularly as you want.

I have some different questions . . . such as:

- What will you never tire of?
- What will you keep doing until the day you die because it's as natural for you as breathing and as joyful as play?
- Who can you not help but be?
- What can you not help but do?

That's what this book is all about, ultimately. *Career Switch* offers a simple, deliberate process to help you achieve the level of clarity that will encourage you to be brave enough to make the career switch your heart has been nagging you to make. This book is about refusing to put up with okayness and competency—meaning, only being pretty good (but not great) when it comes to your career. It's about knowing that how you spend your days working impacts *every* single other thing in your life. It's about knowing that if all of us spent our days doing our ideal work—if we were enthralled by our careers—the world would be a better place.

It's also about *you* knowing, or coming to believe in your heart of hearts, that if you spent *your* days doing work you dream about, *your* world would be a better place.

Switching your career is about committing to doing what seems impossible and to being scared and taking the risk anyway, and being willing to accept the consequences if it doesn't go exactly as planned. It's about being hell bent on not giving up. It's about actually *doing* the work you think you can't do . . .

No matter where.

No matter what.

The Promise of this Book

Go to any bookstore and you'll see rows of career books promising the Holy Grail. I've bought and read nearly every last one of them, hoping I would be able to once and for all put the question, "What should I do with my life?" to bed. That didn't happen. Not for a long time anyway. And when it did, it happened because of the process I am about to share with you in this book. Before we get to that however, let's start with who would benefit most from this book.

This book is for you if you:

- Wake up every day with a nagging sense that time is running out and there's something else you want to be doing, but you aren't sure what that is.

- Feel drained and wiped out at the end of the day from doing a job that may bring you a decent paycheck, but little or nothing in the way of personal satisfaction.

- Have been laid off and are both scared because you aren't sure what's next and thrilled because you know now is the time for you to do something that matters to you . . . and you need help figuring out what that is.

- Wonder what the heck happened to the you that used to be daring and fearless when it came to change because it doesn't at all resemble the you who has been slogging through her work for the past, *ahem,* too many years.

- Kind of, sort of, maybe already know what you want to do, but are too scared to try to succeed at it.

- Have been slowly looking over the edge of the cliff into the water of the unknown below and need a gentle, but firm, push off it.

Who else is this book for? This book is for you if you want to engage in a practical process for helping you reinvent your career, and yourself, and for putting the career question to bed.

Well, that sounds boring actually. This is not boring. This is fun. This book is about getting dirty and not being afraid to look like a mess—and you probably will look like a mess. I sure did when I navigated this career-switching business myself. I was the woman no man would pick, no daughter would want, and no mother would claim. But that's only because when we go through a significant change our madness looks nonsensical to outsiders. The crazy goodness of the process rarely shows itself until we've emerged from the rubble that was our old way of thinking. That's why I wanted to make the process of achieving clarity on your career a playful one.

This is not a book about thinking and hoping and crossing your fingers. It's about writing yourself silly and then taking massive, immediate, and playful action on whatever you discover.

The one caveat is that this book is about writing your way to career clarity (well, writing plus a whole lot of other play, too) so writing should probably be something you enjoy at least as much as a nice hot shower. If you hate the act of writing, this is probably not going to be the best book for you. You don't have to be a writer or have a desire to be a writer, however, to do the writing exercises I'm going to suggest here. There will be no editors or "grammar police" reading what you write. It's actually not possible to do any of this wrong.

What do you need to bring to the process? Honesty, desire for change, commitment, and a desire to have some fun. These are the main qualities you'll have to take on to get as much out of this process as you can. Getting clarity on how you want to switch your career and the kind of work you want to do in the future will take some time. It will take some effort. It will take a willingness to be vulnerable. It will also be well worth it.

Oh, and you'll also need a really great pen. I find I am much smarter and more interesting when I write with great pens. You might be, too.

What this Book Is Not

There are many variables to consider when switching your career, such as how to assess your strengths, how and where to network, how to write a résumé that gets noticed, how to research jobs, and more. Then, once you figure out some of the how to's you have to figure out the steps that will get you from where you are to where you want to be. A definitive work on career change could take thousands of pages. This is *not* that book. I promise it is absolutely not that book.

This book addresses *one* part of the career change process, the part about clarity. It's a tool to help you get clear because once you have clarity and you act on behalf of that clarity, the people in your life, the resources around you, and the world outside will conspire to help you make what you want to happen, happen.

Who Am I to Tell You This?

Let me share a little bit about my background.

I am a former teacher, counselor, and athletic coach turned writer, consummate career switcher and yet to be determined. I have a master's degree in sociology, a master's in counselor education, and I am currently knee deep in my latest educational endeavor. I spent many years teaching and counseling a variety of different populations from incest victims and juvenile offenders, to runaways, gifted adolescents, underprivileged high school students, girls struggling with eating disorders, career changers, and others. When I wasn't doing that, I was hopping to any job that sparked my interest, and writing for anyone who would pay me—and even some who wouldn't. For the past seven years, I have run my own business as a career and business coach, a marketing consultant, a numerologist (yes, really), a freelance writer, a copywriter, and a retreat leader—though not all of those titles at the same time.

We all have our "thing," our life lesson. This is the thing that will show up over and over in every size, shape, and form so that we never forget it or stop learning from it our whole lives long. It's usually not a pretty issue. We can get inflamed and agitated about it, or it can cause us to be manic and over enthused. It usually causes us an inordinate amount of angst and frustration, while at the same time we are drawn to it like a car accident or a horror scene. We are drawn to engage with it, argue with it, and overcome it.

For some people, the issue is money. They have lessons to learn about finances. For others, their lessons have to do with their relationships or weight or health or family. For me, it's the issue of my career—or more specifically, the lessons pertaining to my career choice. This has been the "thing" I've wrestled with since I was fourteen years old.

Career, and more specifically the choices people make that guide the 16 percent of their waking lives spent working, fascinates me.[1] I'm always interested in the choices people make as it relates to their career and why they make them. If we ever meet at a party, I'll ask you about yours—and not in the perfunctory way that many people do. I will want to know how you chose it, when you knew what you wanted to do, how long you've been doing it, and how long you plan to stay with it. As we converse, I won't let you get away with offering me broad sweeps of information. I'll want details.

If you indulge me at all, I won't be able to stop. I'll ask you about the career path of your parents, your significant other, and your best friends. You could feel violated and creeped out by my interest in you and the people you know, or you could be thoroughly excited that a stranger could actually care so much about your life and passions. I hope the latter.

The funny thing is that none of this curiosity and study, as it turns out, has had much of anything to do with my own career satisfaction. I was the quintessential career hopper for years. I spent the first twenty years of my working life going from job to job, career to career, graduate degree to graduate degree, business to business, always feeling like I was close to hitting my mark, and yet not quite landing in the sweet spot. During those years, I didn't allow myself to take my career where I wanted it to go.

As a result, I know that this hopping business can kill a person's spirit. For so many years, my career was guided by what I thought I was *supposed* to do, what I *should* like, what was supposed to *fit* my personality. Yes, I took the assessments and personality tests that are so popular among career guides. The truth is that I wasn't confused. I knew I wanted two, and usually even three, simultaneous careers – one that allowed me to work closely with people and one where I could write until my fingers turned blue; I just didn't have the courage yet to put it on the table in that way, because designing a portfolio career felt too scary, too risky, and too special of a career for me. I felt obligated to pick a lane for my career even though it went against everything my heart was telling me. So I would read about other people in books about career change, wishing I had the courage to choose a focus and make the kind of changes in my life that they were making in theirs. In my career coaching practice I would even coach clients to do what was in their hearts, all while failing to do what was in my heart or achieve the level of satisfaction in my own work that they would subsequently find. Meanwhile my time and my own talents were going to waste. I was a master at dreaming big and playing small.

Finally there came a point when the universe conspired to give me a gigantic slap on the face and I became hell bent on doing work that I loved, work that I cared about, work that made me giddy with joy at the end of the day, and work that didn't require me to pick a lane and stay there. I suspect that point came when I was approaching forty and I had a brief moment where I thought it was too late. Then, in the next minute, I realized that if all went according to plan I still had a solid thirty years left to work, which sounds utterly fabulous, as long as that work happens to be crazy good.

I wasn't exactly sure how I was going to get there, to this crazy good work, but I didn't care anymore. I finally committed to it.

The irony was that in the end, after years of taking career assessments and thousands of dollars spent on therapy and coaches and personality tests, the one tool that gave me the clarity, confidence, and chutzpa I needed to move forward with what I wanted was the exact tool I needed to do the work I dreamed about doing: a pen.

This book is about becoming more of who you are no matter what your path is, something I resisted for so long. I like to think that if this book had been available to me twenty years ago I could have learned the lesson and moved on to something else. But I'm fairly certain that's not how it works. For some reason I needed to spend the first forty years of my life wrestling the question of what to do for a living to the ground with every ounce of strength and energy I had so that I could spend the next forty or more reaping the fruits of the victory of planting my stake in the right, most fertile ground, and then teaching others how to do the same.

Now, in my early forties, I am doing the work I love. I look back on the past twenty years of my working life and I see glimpses of it along the way. I would dip my toe in on occasion. Sometimes I jumped in head first, and then ran out of the pool kicking and screaming. Other times I was content to sit on the edge of the pool wondering what the hell I was waiting for. Finally, going through the process that I am about to share with you allowed me to see what I wanted with new eyes, and as a result, I began to embrace it instead of hide from it. I began to shout it from the rooftops instead of sabotaging my own success, and I stopped giving lip service to my dreams. I made them happen.

I wouldn't have been able to do that if I hadn't taken the most important step of all: getting clear on what I wanted through writing my very first letter to Crazy.

The goal of this book is to help you do the same so that you can contribute the best of who you are to everyone you cross on your path.

Write That Sh*t Down by Hand . . . and for God's Sake, Woman, Be Specific!

"It is not a bad idea to get in the habit of writing down one's thoughts. It saves one having to bother anyone else with them."

—Isabel Colegate

Whenever I need to figure something out or I really want something to happen, I write it down. That may sound a little woo woo (which is why I threw the "shit" in there), but I've tried everything else to get clarity and this is the only thing that works. I've discovered my recipe for success: me, a blank page, a totally cool pen, and the crazy machinations of a mind that never sleeps.

For centuries people have used journals to bring them closer to understanding who they are. A journal serves as a mirror for the soul, a confidant, and a place to express our wildest, uncensored imaginings. Writing changes our moods because it allows us to "reboot": We can unload what is keeping us down and make room for what will lift us up. The mere act of putting pen to paper alters the chemistry in our brain.

When we write, the reticular activation system (RAS) is stimulated. This system acts as a filter for everything our brain needs to process. When we give more focus to something by writing it down, our brain bumps it up on the importance scale. In *Write It Down, Make It Happen*, Henriette Anne Klauser says, "Writing triggers the RAS, which in turn sends a signal to the cerebral cortex: 'Wake up! Pay attention! Don't miss this detail!' Once you write down a goal, your brain will be working overtime to see you get it, and will alert you to the signs and signals that . . . were there all along."[2]

I can still remember my first journal. I called it a diary back then, but it served the same purpose. I used up every square inch of that pink, hardcover, flower-filled vessel of ideas writing about the boys I had a crush on, body image crazi-ness, and the people and events that made up my life at the ripe old age of eight. I was a private, sensitive, and emotional kid, and my journals represented my own secret world. Since then, I have filled hundreds of journals and thousands of pages with my hopes, fears, dreams, gratitude, and everything else I have ever tried to figure out.

I am at once amazed and scared by the power of writing thoughts, ideas, and dreams down. When I write something down, it happens. From jobs to relationships, money, family, and work, I have been writing "letters" in my journals for thirty-plus years.

At the risk of sounding bossy, I think you should write it all down too. So convinced am I that it can create radical change in your life, I have dedicated an entire book to showing you how to do it. Writing letters to something or someone who is showing up in your life and creating a challenge for you is the epitome of practicality and hope. It allows you to get clear, invite that some-thing or someone into a conversation with you—in private—and act it all out in the safety of words. It's a two-dimensional experience that allows you to risk just enough to pretend that what you want is already happening or what you need to do is already being done.

By the way, this process is not about affirmations or pie-in-the-sky wishes. It's a specific, concrete, and in-the-moment process. It's over-the-top empow-ering. This, my friend, is how you're going to discover the work you love to do and the courage inside yourself to pursue it.

Writing my way through has saved me on more than one occasion. Some-times I like to reread them, but more often than not I like to leave the past where it belongs. Generally I am more drawn to celebrate the person I am right in this moment rather than reading about an earlier version of me that was unsure, uncertain, and scared. Sometimes I will see a particular journal and have a physical reaction because I can remember in fine detail where I was when I was writing it, what I was going through, and what I was trying to escape. I don't need to open it. I can picture the pages and the words in my mind. I know the location of all the smears, the rips, and the scribbles. There's a profound comfort in that knowledge. In some ways, those journals are more me than I've ever allowed myself to be.

Over the course of my life I have burned some journals, hidden some, moved some, and lost some. When I was twenty-nine years old, I was packing up my car for a cross-country move. I was moving from Boulder, Colorado, to Charlottes-ville, Virginia, to attend the University of Virginia for graduate school, a goal I had written down so many times that when it actually happened the way I had writ-ten it, it was nearly no surprise at all. Having recently ended a five-year relation-ship, I was simplifying my life and I had a deep desire only to move what could fit in my Subaru Outback.

While I was packing, I came across a box that I had been moving from house to house for over ten years. It was filled with all of my journals. I sat down on the floor and began flipping through them. They were at once comforting and scary. I imagined someone, my parents mostly, finding this box if some-thing ever happened to me and I shuddered. These books were so personal, so deeply private, and even in my death I would never want them to be seen by anyone else, so I decided to get rid of them.

I wrapped the box in a black trash bag and took it to a dumpster behind an old warehouse and let it go. I felt like I was dumping a body: Not that I would know what that would be like, but I had the distinct feeling that I was doing something wrong and I remember looking around to make sure nobody was watching. Of course, as soon as I returned home I wanted them back. I wondered why I didn't opt to get a lockbox that would spontaneously combust upon word of my death. I felt naked without my journals, as though I was walking around with a half a body, apparently the one I had dumped just moments before. Suddenly all of the emo-tions and ideas I thought I had a handle on began to wobble in my mind. Those journals, as private and raw as they were and as rarely as I had reviewed them over the past ten years, were evidence of my personal investment. They reflected my belief that I could figure my life out, change what wasn't working, ask questions, and the world would answer.

Eventually I got over disposing of my journals and actually began to sense that a weight had been lifted. On some level I had been carrying around old thoughts and memories, some that were really not pleasant, like an awkward piece of luggage. By letting them go I had let the past go: one of the most empowering choices anyone can ever make.

Still, I do not believe there is any more powerful practice than writing down what we want, what is in our hearts. When I was talking to my friend one day she said that when she is going through a difficult time she can't bear to look at her journal. Each time she catches a glimpse of it the thought of literally putting pen to paper scares her. She knows that if she writes anything down, she won't be able to hide anymore or be okay with denying the pain she's experiencing.

Although writing is such a simple exercise, it can draw out complexities and layers of emotions that are almost unbearable. When that happens we can be even more confident that engaging with the paper is exactly what we need. That's because when we write it's as if we are admitting control. We may be confused, angry, frustrated, or scared, but writing is an inherently optimistic activity to pursue. We get to have our say and use the imagination to create uncensored, unedited, and improvisational dreams that remind us of how powerful we are.

In writing this book, I was drawn to review some of my old journals, and I was blown away by what I found. In one journal entry, dated February 12, 2006, I wrote:

Dear Melani,

What do you want to be known for?
I want to write a book or books about career that help people get unstuck and go after what they want. I want to help people reinvent themselves with style. I want to be seen as an expert on career choice and career reinvention, and I want to spend my days writing about it. I want to speak to college students and recent grads, and I want to teach them how to use what they are good at and never waste time. I want to give workshops to women over forty who feel stuck so they can have a safe

space to get unstuck and build a community around them where they
can take the risks and the leaps of faith they've secretly been dreaming
about. I want ideas to flow freely, for resources to show up, and to accom-
plish my dream of becoming an author by writing about how others can
achieve their career dreams. I want my writing to be useful and helpful. I
want it to matter. I want my daughter to be proud of me.

My daughter was still the size of a sea monkey in my belly at the time I wrote that journal entry, and I remember feeling the urgency of getting all of that to happen by the time she was born later that summer. Not all of it did, but some of it did.

The rest is now.

When you write a dream or a goal down, you call attention to it. You make it important, and, as a result, people in your life and the forces you don't even realize exist begin to conspire in your favor to make it happen. In truth, it happens so effortlessly that, as was the case with my friend, sometimes I actually get scared to write my thoughts, dreams and hopes down. When I write them down I have to get out of the way, do my work and simply let the fruits of that intention come to me.

When I signed a contract with my editor for her work on this book I sent her a check that freaked me out a little bit. I had this book in my head for seven years and yet this was the first time I'd ever made a true commitment to it. This was at a time when I had recently lost all of my monthly income, so not only was I spending money I didn't have, I was also declaring to the universe that I was going to write my book by the end of the year.

As soon as the contract was signed, I sat down and wrote a letter to the money.

Dear Money,

I paid you today. I am scared of you. You intimidate me, like I should
be better than I am if I am going to make a commitment like this. You

have made me doubt myself, so I need you to do something for me. If I promise to write every day, put in the hours, and do my very best, no holding back, will you please come back to me?

After I wrote the letter, I wrote down all of the reasons I had for writing the book and all of the resources I would need to get together in my life—both financially and emotionally—to make it happen without negatively impacting my family. I committed to follow through on my promise. Later that same day I put out the word about my recently revived freelance writing and copywriting business, and within twelve hours the equivalent amount of money I'd sent to my editor was back in my bank account.

Was the return of the money partly due to the fact that I was proactive and put some marketing activities in motion in my business? Absolutely. This is not a book about some airy-fairy practice of just floating ideas out into the universe and having results land in your lap without effort. But had I not written the letter, specifically describing what I wanted and when I needed it to happen, or responded quickly to the opportunities that I set in motion, then the chances that that money would have come back to me, especially that quickly, would've been slim.

I have hundreds, if not thousands, of examples of what can happen when you put pen to paper and get specific about what you want to happen. Whenever my husband and I are struggling to achieve some clarity on an issue or there's an outcome we really want, I always tell him I need to go and "write that sh*t dooooown." Over the years he has seen how I am able to create results from my efforts, and that sometimes my route can get a little confused or the timing a little slow therefore he always now says, "Yeah, go do that. But for God's sakes, woman, be specific!" Don't just ask for money, ask for $3,000 dollars *by the end of the week.*

How you spend your days is one of the most important decisions you make, and the cool thing is that you are asked to make it every single day. No matter what you are doing today, if you hate it you don't have to do it again tomorrow. You don't have to settle for a lifetime of doing work you hate or that bores you. You don't have to sit back and waste your talents. You don't have to watch others live lives of significance, influence, passion, and/or success while you sit back and dream. You can have that in your career, too.

Your ideal work, your ideal life, can start with a simple, specific letter that helps you gain clarity over an issue with which you're wrestling.

How to Use this Book

Before we get to your first letter I want to give you a little bit of guidance on how to implement my advice and procedures.

The book is designed to give structure to a process (in this case, getting clarity on your career) that otherwise can take you off track and make you feel like you're going deeper and deeper into a rabbit hole with no signs of light. Starting a new career after being out of the work force for years or making a dramatic change while you're still living with a working identity that's old and outdated requires a lot of thought and execution. And it could well take longer than you imagine it will. However, if you stick with these letters you will gain the clarity you are looking for, and you will do it more quickly than if you try to wing it and see what happens.

As I've said, this process requires equal amounts of inner work and outer work. Doing the inner work will you help you plant your feet on the ground. But if you only look inside you'll quickly become stuck in the quicksand. By doing only the inner work you run the risk of fooling yourself into believing that the answers lie solely in your head. If you can't get to the answer that way then you'll end up waiting for the clouds to part rather than engage in the type of action that will help you find your way.

Enter the letters, a solution to the aforementioned dilemma. There are sixteen letters in this book and each chapter is structured in the same way. Each one begins with a focus on a specific topic, which is addressed via stories, research, and information. Then you will complete a section called "Priming the Pump," designed to warm you up and help you focus on what is going on in-the-moment. Next is the "Write That Sh*t Down" section, where you will write a letter or letters designed to draw attention to the issue at hand, and help you articulate what you want without reservation and without judgment, identify the people in your life who can help you, and spur you into action.

Next you will be given some suggestions for how to "Play with It." Finally at the end of each chapter you will be guided to a website where you'll find a short writing exercise designed to review what you did in the chapter and keep you accountable for what you have written about in your letters.

Because of the intensity of the exercises and the expectation that you do something as a result of the information you get from writing, this book is not meant to be devoured in a single sitting. If it is, then you aren't taking the action required to make significant changes happen in your career. Here's one possible way to approach it: Read a chapter, do all of the suggested exercises, and then give yourself some time to reap the rewards of your efforts before you move on to the next. That could be anywhere from forty-eight hours to two weeks, depending on how quickly you are able to put all of the suggestions into practice.

Many books on career change are filled with lengthy case studies, so that may be what you're used to. This book is not set up that way. There are a few snippets from letters I or others have written when I thought they would be helpful to include, but these are few and far between.[3] That's because, while it can be helpful to hear how others have navigated a similar transition, it's also possible to waste time living through the stories of others and comparing your experience to them in a way that stops you in your tracks. That's often what takes my clients out. I can relate. Over the years I've read too many career books to count, and the result was that I often felt even further away from what I wanted to do than when I started. Or at least further away from the belief that I could do it after comparing myself to so many others who I read about on those pages who seemed more special than I was. It wasn't until I approached this process as if I were blazing the trail of career reinvention, and decided to own each and every step of the way by blocking out whatever everyone else said I should or shouldn't do and what I should or shouldn't want, that I was able to create the breakthrough I needed.

Let this book be about you. We all have different parts to play and we have to give ourselves the chance to play them.

There is a reason for the progression and flow of the letters, so I encourage you to take on the process and stick with it. As a former counselor, I always used to say to my clients, "Stick with the process." No matter who you are, how successful you've become, or how self-aware you are, when you're going through the type of inner and outer work that requires "putting yourself out there" and being completely honest about what you feel and what you want, it's easy to get taken out. You'll feel uncomfortable, vulnerable, and exposed, and at some point you'll probably want to quit. You'll want to go back to a place that's safe so you can take risk and the possibility of failure out of the equation. This makes sense! But I know that if you're reading this you want more from yourself. So give yourself this gift, and promise yourself that you're going to stick with it. If you do, when it's time to go knocking on the door of your ideal work it will say, "Hi. I've been waiting for you. C'mon in."

WRITE THAT SH*T DOWN

When you come to the end of every chapter, I will give you two writing exercises. The first is an exercise to prime the pump. The second is a letter.

Let's Get the Ball Rolling: Priming the Pump

In this book, I am going to walk you through the sixteen letters I wrote that allowed me, for the first time in my life, to put the career question to bed. (At least for now. I know I still have many career switches ahead of me.) These are the letters that took me from confused, scared, defeated, uninspired, and unmotivated to waking up excited, committed, and enthralled by my work and the life it affords me. You will notice that my early letters focus almost exclusively on my desire to write. As I became more clear and moved further through the process I realized that was only a part of my career dream. Had I not stuck with it, I probably would still be caught up fantasizing about a career I don't really want at all, at least not in the way I thought I did. So, trust you will find the clarity you seek.

This book is not about chasing money or accumulating riches. It's not about living a life of success. Rather it's about living a life of significance. If money follows (and I sure hope it does), then that's fabulous, of course, but more than anything else *Career Switch* is about finding clarity and meaning in a world that appears intent on helping us lose our way all in the name of goods we don't want or need, status that is meaningless, and success that's been defined for us by others.

Before we dig in to the Big Sixteen, we need to start with the most important letter of them all. This letter will set the stage for the entire process. It will put all of the wheels securely in motion and place the wind at your back. Please get ready to write it now.

All you need is a comfortable location, a favorite pen, a blank page, a timer, and thirty minutes to yourself.

For the first part of this exercise, set your timer for two minutes. On your blank sheet of paper, write down every word that comes to your mind as it relates to your career. These can be about a feeling, a thing, a thought, a person, a place, whatever. Write for two minutes straight.

Go.

When you're finished, take a minute to review your list of words. What do they tell you about where you are right now? Are you excited? Scared? Curious? Motivated? Optimistic? Doubtful? Energized?

Now, set your timer for another two minutes. This time write down whatever theme emerged from your first list. Don't worry about *why* you think it emerged, simply focus on the *what*. Be an anthropologist rather than an analyst.

Go.

Doing these two exercises is called "priming the pump." Priming the pump is a practice that can warm you up, help you settle in to how you are feeling right now, and open you up so you can write a letter from a place of peace and strength. We'll do this again and again throughout the book. It's a calming mechanism that allows you to clear whatever is inflamed or agitated or excessive in your mind so you are free to write what is in your heart.

Write a Letter to Yourself

Now, let's move on to your important first letter.

Take a deep breath. Look at a new blank page in front of you. It is a gift. It represents freedom, hope, dreams, and unlimited possibility. This is your book about your work life, your career. You get to design your path. There are no roadblocks. No speed bumps. No traffic lights. You can make it as easy as you want to. You get to have what you want; you just have to get specific about it before it will come to you.

This first letter is going to be a letter to Yourself. Read the prompt I have given you, and then take as much time as you need to write the letter. There is no right way to do it. The only rule is that you keep writing. Grammar doesn't matter. Structure doesn't matter. The only thing that matters is that you write the truth. Always write the truth.

Dear (insert your name),

I am doing this because . . .

Go.

Congratulations! Your first letter is complete and you've made a commitment to a process designed solely to help you gain clarity on your career. In the chapters that follow you will be asked to look at your life and career from many different angles and respond to what you discover by writing letters and then acting on behalf of what you've written. My hope is that you'll find this process as helpful as I did and as many of my clients have, and that by the end you'll be knocking on the door of your career dream.

Chapter 1
I Wrote a Letter to Crazy and Permission Wrote Me Back

"Let us watch well our beginnings, and results will manage themselves."

—Alexander Clark

In early 2006 I decided to hang out my shingle as a career coach and blogger and try my hand at running my own business. I thought for sure that with my credentials, experience, and training I would have no problem attracting all of the clients I needed to fill my practice. I learned quickly that my business had very little to do with the service I was able to provide and everything to do with how well I was marketing those services.

As a former teacher, counselor, and coach, I had zero interest or training in marketing. What I did have training in, however, was human behavior, relationships, and writing, so I quickly built up a practice that was based nearly 100 percent on referrals and people who found me through my writing. Due to my success in building a practice without having to employ many of the tactics that people in the helping professions fear having to do themselves, eventually other coaches, therapists, and consultants started coming to me for help with their writing and marketing. While all I really wanted to do at the time was to write about work and careers, I was seduced by the money I could make teaching people how to market their businesses better so they could make more money, thus my business began to change. Pretty soon I was a full-fledged marketing consultant. Writing about career and leading retreats were fun time fillers that I did on the side.

By December 2008, my marketing business was doing well, but I hated the work. Great set up, right? Spending twelve hours a day doing work I didn't enjoy was burning me out. I was exhausted from taking on clients who weren't a fit for me, and I was tired of the grind of marketing myself 24/7 to do more of the work I didn't like doing. I was also upset for allowing myself to get so far off track from doing the work I had set out to do in the first place.

I wanted out. Unfortunately, instead of pausing and re-evaluating my situation, what I did was dive deeper into that work.

In the midst of contemplating what I was going to do to change direction, I received a phone call and learned that my mother had been in a horrible car accident. She was being airlifted to the hospital. We didn't know if she was going to make it. Fortunately, she did, with a ruptured spleen, a broken pelvis, a fracture in her vertebrae, and six broken ribs, among other complications. She was going to need a lot of help—my help. I spent the next several weeks taking care of my mom as she transitioned out of the hospital and began her rehabilitation at home.

While I was there, I received an email from someone who wanted to hire me as a marketing consultant. I remember talking to my dad about it and really struggling over whether or not I should do it. I was excited on the one hand, because I knew it was going to provide more income stability for me and I would still be able to maintain my freedom and flexibility, which was at the forefront of my mind while I was helping my mom. On the other hand, the visceral reaction I felt when I thought about saying yes was profound. I had a heavy lump in my heart and I remember a moment when my throat literally constricted. I felt certain that if I accepted the contract being offered I would once again be walking further away from what I really wanted. In doing so, I would be sending a powerful message to my subconscious mind that I don't get to do what I want, that doing what one really wants to do is a dream reserved for others.

In the end, I picked security over love. I ignored the signs my body was giving me and took on the client. Immediately after I did so I resented that I wasn't doing the work I had originally intended to do and I was frustrated with myself for allowing money to be my primary driver. And boy was I good at justifying my decision. *I have to make this much money because I need to give my daughter more*, I thought. *I have to make this much money because we have a new house and my daughter goes to an expensive day care. We want to go on vacation and our grocery bills are high, and blah blah blah.*

To make up for how much I hated my day-to-day work, I kept up my blog on career and personal development, co-hosted Mojo Retreats and saw counseling clients on the side. I also tested out other careers to see what stuck. And while that is where I derived my excitement and satisfaction, I had convinced myself that the money I would receive from doing work I truly loved would never be "enough." In addition, I continued to hear the voice in my head say, "Pick a lane!" and I eventually started to believe it.

I lived that ways for four years and it took a dramatic toll on me. I was sick a lot. I was cranky. I hated work. I rarely slept through the night. I felt stuck. And all of my free time was spent wondering how I was going to get out of it. By that time I had so many stories keeping me tied to that work that I sabotaged every window of opportunity I had to get out.

My story was that my family and I could not live without my income and if I walked away from it then I would somehow be releasing claim to any and all future earnings. To not make money today meant to not make money tomorrow.

I believed that I would let people down. People with excessive education and licenses to practice practical work that provides reasonably good and steady income do not quit their job to "see what happens." In my mind that was immature, irresponsible, and self-indulgent.

I believed that unless I was the best at what I wanted to do then I had no business even trying. I had to be extraordinary if I was going to try and switch my career.

I believed that I wouldn't be able to explain the choice if it didn't work out. I worried I might have to crawl back to the work I'd vowed I'd never do again.

I believed all of those thoughts and they drove my decision to stay doing that work. Until one day when I decided that the only way I was going to be okay was if I took a major step toward what I had wanted to do when I originally hung out that shingle in the first place.

So I did.

I stopped working with all but one of my clients, I shut down my blogs, I took down information products related to marketing and growing your business, I deleted my Twitter and YouTube account, un-friended about 4,000-plus people on Facebook and tried to erase every single sign of myself online as a marketing consultant. (When it comes to reinvention, I don't fool around.)

I began sleeping more, writing more, playing more, and feeling like myself again. I started feeling optimistic and unstoppable again. I started getting my confidence back and taking more chances. And as cliché as it may sound, I finally found my voice again.

Once that happened, I was able to see the work I had been doing as a marketing consultant for what it really was. A paycheck I felt obligated to claim. Once I acknowledged that I could be honest about what a poor fit it was and that while I was very proud of what I had been able to build, because it didn't fit my personality and I didn't love it, there was only so far I was going to be able to take it.

Eventually it became clear that my work with the client I had kept was heading in the wrong direction but while I should have quit, my fear of losing all of that income and not having a sure way of replacing it right away kept me going.

However, the letter that brought me to the point of no return was a letter I wrote to Crazy. By this point I had reached the end of my rope. I felt unchallenged, bored, and pent up. I was doing inane tasks; my talents, skills, experience and education were going to waste; and with each day that went by, I was moving further away from doing work that I wanted to do. My dreams were becoming more and more distant and the worst part about it is that I was letting it happen. My daughter was feeling my lack of joy, my husband was feeling it, and my friends were feeling it.

So, I wrote a letter to Crazy. Here's what it said.

Dear Crazy,

I am going to quit all of the work I am doing with this client and focus on my writing full time. I am going to give up all of my current income, the income that keeps my daughter in private school, allows our family to take regular vacations, makes it easy not to worry about large grocery bills and frequent nights out, and that never gives me a heart attack when the air conditioner breaks or I get a monster dentist bill. I am going to do all of this without backup income or backup clients. I am just going to do it and see what happens, because if I don't I might lose my mind and not get it back.

It feels irresponsible and shortsighted, and totally inappropriate, but maybe it's about time for all of that to come to pass. I have wanted to write for a living since I was 20 years old. Probably before. I am sick of being safe. I am sick of bending. I am sick of not giving myself enough credit to go after what I want. I am sick of listening to advice on the "right thing to do." I am sick of going down the rabbit holes of convention and living up to other people's expectations. I am sick of believing all of the people who tell me that what I want to do is a pipe dream. I am sick of letting my safe, rational, uptight self control the me who speaks in a whisper, but is far more compelling. I am sick of ignoring the me that knows me better than anyone else.

I am going to quit soon. Really soon. I can't wait, but I am scared, too. Though not too scared to give myself a do-over.

I am going to do this.

And, Crazy, I want to write and for it to be really great.

What do you think?

Melani

Not twenty-four hours after I wrote the letter, my client who I had worked with for over three and half years fired me. The Universe decided it was no longer going to wait for me to do what I should have done years before. It was exactly what needed to happen and my career was thrilled.

That afternoon, I opened up my freelance writing business . . . again.

I didn't have much of a financial reserve. I didn't have any so-called ducks in a row, but I felt so free that I didn't care. For the first time in years I stopped creating moneymaking distractions and followed my heart and the work that lit me up more than anything else.

The surprising part of getting fired and being faced with a clear calendar for the first time in seven years was that all of the horrible things I had predicted would happen never did. I didn't become invisible. I didn't become less interesting or less intelligent. I didn't end up on the street. I just stopped doing that particular job and followed my heart.

Letting everything else go and committing to my writing was probably the craziest thing I have ever done, especially now that I know that writing is just one part of my career dream puzzle. It was crazier than backpacking in the woods for a month, crazier than jumping out of an airplane, crazier than running an ultra-marathon, crazier than all of the other crazy stuff I've done. I had many moments when I thought, "Who do I think I am to be so selfish, to risk so much so I can do what I want and love, not knowing if it will ever work out?" What I realized by going through this process, however is that the career you want or the job you dream about more often than not is waiting for you to be *ready enough*.

It's kind of like having children. People who don't have children talk a lot about getting "ready" to have them. They want to be in the right place financially or they want to have more "things" in place so it can all go according to plan. Anyone with kids will tell you, you are *never* ready. There is no such thing as the most perfect and opportune time; however, as soon as it happens it becomes the right time. One day you are not ready at all, and the next day when you are staring at the plus sign on the home pregnancy test you are as ready as you could possibly be. You are ready because you have to be, and while the fear about the unknown may stick around, you realize that the fear is not nearly as important as having the kid you want.

When it comes to your career, once you commit to a path with your whole heart, and dive in the deep end of the pool, you will be more than ready enough to make it all happen.

Taking the Leap

There is a way to accept fear and include it as part of your experience so that you can move forward with what you want despite its presence. I have learned to accept my fear through writing letters first, and taking action on the content of those letters second.

To illustrate how letter writing is one way to get at, and overcome the stories we tell ourselves, I'm going to share the story of one of my clients, a woman named Molly.

Molly was a forty-one-year old, former estate-planning lawyer turned stay-at-home mom to two boys. She had originally planned to keep working when her first son was born. But as soon as she bounced back to work after her maternity leave she found herself fighting with her boss about taking time off and feeling slighted by coworkers who resented her new "lifestyle." To make matters worse, she didn't even like the work she was doing. She was burned out and uninspired. Having her son put all of the work she was doing into perspective, and she realized her job wasn't providing her the kind of life she wanted anymore.

When Molly had her second child, she decided to take a three-year "leave" to stay at home with her kids full time. It was a huge financial shift and her entire family felt the loss of income, nonetheless she and her husband worked it out. However, by the time her third child was about to arrive, Molly spiraled into panic mode. Her leave was about to run out and even though she didn't really want to go back to her job, she was scared to give up her spot at her firm without a new plan in place. She had relished the time she had at home, and while spending time with her babies confirmed she had made the right decision originally to leave her job and take a break from working in the traditional sense, she also had a nagging feeling that there was something she was supposed to be doing and wasn't. She felt grateful that she had been able to stay at home with her kids. At the same time, she really wanted to find work that meant something to her. She and her husband wanted to increase their family income so they could buy the house they wanted, take more vacation trips, and comfortably send their kids to a private school; but, Molly needed to feel fulfilled, too.

Molly came to me because she felt overwhelmed and out of control. She had ideas about what she wanted to do, ideas she hadn't shared with anyone else, but they all felt too impossible and impractical for her taste. Someone referred her to me because of my background as a career coach and my experience as a marketing consultant, since Molly had some ideas about starting her own business venture.

Here's how our first conversation unfolded.

Me: Can you tell me a little bit about what brought you here today?

Molly: I think I'm here because I feel guilty.

Me: Guilty about what?

Molly: Guilty because I love my kids, but I also really want to work.

Me: Are those mutually exclusive?

Molly: No, but I feel bad for wanting to work, like I'm a bad mother for wanting to work.

Me: Do you think that mothers who work, and who *like* to work are bad mothers?

Molly: No. I guess part of it is that I feel like what I want to do is silly, and so farfetched, that because I have kids who need me I shouldn't get to try for it.

Me: What do you mean by "get" to try for it? It sounds like you're looking for permission. Is that true?

Molly: Probably. In a way. Maybe I just want someone to tell me it's okay to want to work and it's okay to give it a try, and that it's okay if I try and it doesn't work out.

Me: Someone like whom? Maybe your husband?

Molly: No, he's very supportive and says he's behind me all the way. And I actually believe him.

Me: Is it maybe your parents or a friend?

Molly: No. I don't think so. I have a great support group around me.

Me: Anyone else come to mind?

Molly: No. But once you said the word "permission" it really struck me, so that must mean something, right?

Me: It's possible. Let's try this. I'd like you to take fifteen minutes tonight and write a letter to Permission. Tell Permission what you want, what you're feeling, and what you want from it. Don't worry about writing perfectly or getting it right. Just set your timer for fifteen minutes and write whatever comes to your mind.

I talked to Molly the next day, and she shared a snippet of her letter with me.

Dear Permission,

I usually feel so confident. I did really well in school. I was good at my job. I think I am a good mom. But for some reason I am really scared to take a chance and change careers. I've never done any work like this before. I don't know if I would be any good at it. What happens if I bomb? What if I take this time away from my kids to pursue it and I fail? Isn't it selfish just to test something out when I have kids at home who need me? Am I tool old to experiment?

I need to know that it's okay for me to do this. Can you tell me it's okay? How will I know it's okay when I don't even know whose permission I am seeking? But I clearly need it. It's like I just want someone with authority to come wave a magic wand over me and tell me this is an okay thing to do and that I am capable of pulling it off. Is that it? Is this all about capability? Do I actually doubt that I can do this? No. I know I can do this. Maybe I need to start doing the work so that I can get feedback from someone in the industry that my work is good. Maybe if I got a thumbs-up from someone in the field that would be all the permission I need. But I can't get that unless I do it . . .

Molly

Molly said that what came up for her while she was writing the letter were all of the stories she had been telling herself about why she couldn't do what she wanted.

From risking loss of income to letting her family down to not knowing how to do it to being a bad mom to failing, Molly had been telling herself all of the stories that would keep her safe. When she wrote the letter to Permission, she realized that all she needed to do was to take a few steps. By taking these few steps it would be impossible for all of her fears to come true. They were really part of an elaborate fantasy she was spinning for herself in the name of safety and comfort.

For most of us, what we do for work significantly impacts not only us but also the people we're closest to. Whether it is our parents, who may have paid for our education; our partners or spouses, who rely on us to share the financial load in our homes; or our kids, who need us to be there and provide for them financially and emotionally, when it comes to our work we don't choose it in a vacuum. Therefore when we want to make a change, we often feel the need to get permission from others. The reality, however, is that no amount of encouragement or permission from others will make a bit of difference if we don't grant ourselves the permission we're looking for first.

For years I dreamed about shutting my marketing consulting business down and the primary reason I kept *dreaming* about walking away from it instead of actually walking away was because I didn't have the permission to do it. I assumed my husband would never go for it, I assumed my parents would be appalled at my decision to give up such a well-paying gig, and I thought that until someone came by with their almighty wand and told me I was a good enough writer now to pursue it more fiercely I had to stay right where I was. Then one day, in an attempt to figure out what was holding me back and what I thought needed to happen before I would get to do what I want, I wrote a letter to Permission.

Here's part of that letter.

Dear Permission,

I'm not sure why but apparently I've decided that I don't GET to do what I want. I have this incessant voice in my head that screams at me every time I make a move toward it by saying any number of totally gut wrenching bits of wisdom such as . . .

- *"You're not a good enough writer."*
- *"Very few people are good enough to make a living writing and you aren't one of them."*
- *"You'll starve."*
- *"It'll never work."*
- *"You have no credentials. No M.F.A. no Ph.D., no bylines, no nothing."*

I am in the habit of believing all of them.

When I pretend not to believe them, then I conveniently come up with some reasons why I really don't want to be a writer, which is simply my attempt to protect myself. I am a master at protecting myself from humiliation, which is what I am pretty certain would be the result of me pursuing my writing, evidenced by the voice inside me that relentlessly repeats that I'll never be good enough.

Damn this is a shitty cycle of lies and self-doubt.

I can't imagine that it is as easy as just wanting permission to do it but now that I write that I think it is. But here's the totally impossible thing about that: I want permission from this imaginary permission granter who grants exclusively to writers. But how could this "person" give me permission if I'm not giving it anything to judge me on? No, a blog does not count. Marketing materials and copywriting clips don't count.

Cripes! Are you so scared to fail that you really won't even start?

Okay, enough. There is no permission granter, so I am going to be it.

I hereby grant you permission to put every last piece of energy you have into trying to make writing for a living a reality. You can do it.

Go. Write for crying out loud. You have been talking about it for over twenty years. Stop dipping your toe in. Jump!

Melani

Further along in the letter I made a list all of the people from whom I thought I needed permission to make it happen: everyone from my parents to my daughter, my husband, my writing teachers, and more. It was a ghastly list that made me realize that by keeping all of their voices in the back of my head as my little puppeteers, the only permission I was giving myself was permission to keep putting it off.

The crazy thing, of course, is that none of them agreed to be on that panel. I put them there because that made my life easier.

Maybe you do the same thing, too. Maybe you have been putting up imaginary barriers that make it impossible for you to go after your ideal work and you don't even realize it. Maybe, if you wrote your own letter to Permission you would gain an insight about the kind of beliefs or behaviors that stop you.

Maybe you will learn you are your single greatest barrier to success. Or maybe you will learn that others have been happily (or often even reluctantly) given the power to decide what you can and cannot do.

Then maybe you will see how quickly the power dynamic can change and pretty soon the idea of permission will be off the table. You will just do it because it's what you want.

In Molly's case, after she was able to see that the story she was spinning was flawed, she decided to take the few steps she needed to test whether or not she was capable of doing the work she wanted. She had a secret dream of becoming a writer in the finance industry. With a background in estate planning, a passion for finance, and a love for writing, she imagined a world where she could blend everything she loved to do and still be home and available to her kids. She reached out to her contacts and, before she knew it, she had three writing assignments, all of which were given rave reviews.

This is what she wrote me in a follow-up email.

Melani,

Thank you for encouraging me to write a letter to Permission. It felt silly at first, but the more I wrote the more I realized that I was acting far more committed to quashing my dream than I was to bringing it to life. I thought I needed someone to tell me I was good, but I'm pretty sure I already knew that. What I really needed to do more than anything was to give myself permission. Even when my first two assignments came back and the people raved about them, I realized that all of the kudos they gave me were nothing in comparison to the gift of permission I gave myself to keep going forward.

I'm not pretending this work is easy. I work hard to get clients and I write a lot at all times of the day and night so that I can bring in a good income and have time with my family. But there is nothing else I would rather be doing. Whenever I have a slow week or a slow month, of which I have definitely had my share, I inevitably question whether or not I get to keep doing this, and I always go back to that letter I wrote to Permission. The letter helps me to remember that, yes, of course I do.

Molly

WRITE THAT SH*T DOWN

Now it's time for you to play with these ideas.

Priming the Pump

Take a moment to reflect back on your life and all of the critical choices you have made. Set the timer for five minutes and make a list of all of the times you waited to move forward on something until you received permission from someone else. Maybe it was permission to go to a certain school, quit a job, marry the "right" guy, move to a different state, cut your hair, and so on.

Go.

Write a Letter to Permission

Now that you have made a list of all of the times you have sought permission outside of yourself, you are ready to write a letter to Permission as it relates to the big career decision that is challenging you right now.

What do you need to give yourself permission to do? What promises can you make to yourself as it relates to permission? For example, "I give my self permission not to have to be perfect. Not to have to get it right all of the time and to take one step at a time."

How will you know when you've truly granted the permission or what has to happen in order for you to give it to yourself.

Go.

Play with It

Now that you've given yourself permission on paper, it's time to put it into play. You may decide that in order to really take on this new freedom you've given yourself to do what you want that you need to be completely honest with your husband, wife, or significant other about what you want and your plans to make it happen. This doesn't mean they are going to like it or even support it, but it will begin a conversation that will hopefully open both of you up to some new possibilities while you get to try on a new level of confidence and resolve.

Maybe putting this into practice will involve going to your boss and telling him or her that you really want to move into a certain division, and listing out all of the reasons why and how you believe you would contribute in a new role.

Perhaps you will decide to spend tomorrow looking for opportunities to volunteer in the new industry in which you want to work, sending yourself and the Universe a powerful message that you are serious: Now that you have permission, there will be no stopping you from continuing to move forward toward the dream.

Testing it out is a critical piece in this process, as it is with every letter. You can *know* something certainly but until you actually *use* that knowledge, you might as well not know it at all.

So, the question I have for you is, *Now that you have given yourself permission, what are you going to do about it?*

Priming the Pump Part 2

One of my favorite writing prompts involves writing about my *escape dream*. I learned it while I was studying career counseling and it has always stayed with me. When you write about your escape dream, what you'd want above everything else, you bring to the surface powerful clues about something you really need. If you're missing something in your life, whether it is solid connections with other people, something that challenges you and pushes you, or even money, that thing will show up in this dream.

Consider this question: What is your escape dream?

Set your time for ten minutes.

Go.

Write a Letter to Crazy

Now it's your turn to let it all go. When I write my letters to Crazy (and I assure you I have written many), it's astonishing what I learn from the exercise. The really cool thing about these letters is that what feels crazy and impossible in our heads becomes exciting and possible once it's down on paper.

For years I kept the crazy dream of being a writer in my head because I thought it was impossible. It seemed so out of the question that I never even allowed myself to write it down. Once I did, not only did I realize it was possible, but I also saw that there was a lot more to it and that writing was not the only thing I wanted to do. Seeing all of that written down in black and white created an enormous amount of urgency around pursuing my ideas. I no longer spent energy worrying what would happen if my career ideas didn't work, but instead focused all of my energy on doing everything I knew how to do to make them happen. For so long having the belief that it would never work was far more important to me than having the belief that it could. Once I wrote it down, I flipped that mental script instantly.

Now it's your turn. With your journal or a blank piece of paper in front of you, take a few deep breaths. Then consider: What do you really want to do?

Let your vision of this dream career be big and bold and true. Don't hold back because of doubts or other imagined outcomes. Also, ignore all of the shoulds and can'ts that happen to show their ugly faces right when you start to put pen to paper.

What do you really want for yourself?

Set your timer for ten to fifteen minutes.

Dear Crazy . . .

Go.

Play with It

Sometimes your letter to Crazy may be just that, crazy. I have written letters to Crazy over the years that talk about how badly I want to be a professional athlete or study acting and be in movies, or join the FBI, and once I write it all out I realize that I am never going to have those careers. That's okay. In a way it's an exercise that also allows us to let go of former dreams that no longer match who we are or the kind of life we want to lead. In that case, writing it down gets them out of the way and frees us up to move forward on other dreams we want to make happen right now. It helps us to let go of our regrets about paths not taken.

If however, like me and my letter to Crazy, your letter to Crazy reveals something that at one time felt impossible, but now feels entirely necessary, then act on it. If your letter to Crazy revealed that more than anything you want to be invited by *The Today Show* to appear as a guest to talk about your newly released book or the work you are doing, then start figuring out how you can put a compelling media campaign together and give yourself some target dates. Hire a PR expert, or if you need to start smaller, call up the local university and offer an internship to students in the media department to help you get local press and speaking gigs.

To get closer to my crazy writing dream I wrote another letter to Crazy that detailed everything I wanted to happen with the writing side of my career and all of the resources I would need to make it happen. After that I called an editor I had wanted to work with for a long time and told her my ideas for a book. She listened, told me how she could help me achieve my goals, and agreed to do whatever she could to help. With her support I moved faster than I ever would have on my own and I finished a book that I had wanted to write for seven years.

The real value in writing the letter to Crazy is that you realize that you have it in you to turn crazy into reality once you write it down. Words have the power to make an idea or a goal that seems really big and complicated seem simple and straightforward.

Writing a letter to Crazy is something you can do on a regular basis, and from it continue to gain insight and inspiration. Just remember, the key to achieving the results you want is to combine the practice of writing shit down with taking action.

After you complete your letters and before you begin the next chapter, be sure to head over to www.careerswitch.org/1review to get some more writing prompts and review what you've discovered so far.

Chapter 2
I Wrote a Letter to Regret and
Opportunity Wrote Me Back

"Never look back unless you are planning to go that way."
—Henry David Thoreau

In 1995 there was a man living in Liverpool who played the same set of lottery numbers every week. One week, when he failed to renew his ticket, his numbers came in. His distress over losing what he thought was millions of dollars (a fact he actually ended up being wrong about), was so unbearable that he committed suicide.

That is real regret. The kind of regret that happens when we see the difference between how a situation is and how it could have been had we made a different choice.

Imagine if you were offered a trip back in time so you can undo your biggest regret. If you could live your life all over again, what's the one thing you would do differently?

When I ask myself that question, the words shoot out of my mouth without even thinking: my educational and career choices.

It turns out I'm not alone. In the book *If Only* (Broadway, 2005), author Neale J. Roese, Ph.D., cites a series of studies conducted by independent researchers who were interested in finding out what adults consider their biggest regrets. During the period of 1989--2003, adults of all ages were asked the questions: If you could go back and live your life all over again, what would you do differently? What parts of your life would you change? With eleven studies in all, the researchers discovered that the following four regrets appear consistently at the top of the list, in this order, in study after study.[1]

Education: 32 percent
Career: 22 percent
Intimacy: 15 percent
Parenting: 11 percent

This is not so say that the majority of people are unhappy and full of regret. Rather, these are the areas where people see the most need (and room) for improvement.

In the studies, the researchers learned that when it came to regretting a career choice, sometimes the regret focused on wishing they had made the kind of choices that would have led them to have a better career, and other times it was focused on wishing they had spent less time on their career, primarily because it impacted intimacy and parenting, two other top-of-the-list regrets. Education and career were closely tied together in the results, as most people wished they had paid more attention in school or had chosen a different educational path, because of how those choices ended up impacting their careers.

Career choice can be a particularly long-lasting regret. This is partly because there are so many decisions that make up our career story (everything from choosing a major in college to accepting our first job after we graduate from school). So, when a career doesn't turn out like we wanted it to, we can identify various points along the road where we could have taken a turn better suited to us and we didn't. That's hard to swallow. It's also a fairly blurry regret because when it comes to our careers it's never just about picking between two clear paths, it's usually about figuring out a way through a maze full of possible options. I suspect this is why people love career tests: They want to be told there is a single best path, or at least a best two or three, so that their chances of choosing a good fit significantly increase. We don't like to get our lives wrong.

Since you're reading this book right now, it's possible that you have some regrets about choices you made in the past that you believe are preventing you from moving forward. Possibly you say to yourself:

- *I have no idea what I want to do and I clearly made the wrong choice before so what makes me think I'll get it right this time?*
- *It's too late to go for what I really want now.*
- *I guess I just have to live with my mistakes.*
- *If only I could have a do-over.*

If that sounds like you, then keep reading. If you don't have a single regret about the educational or career choices you've made, then hop on over to Chapter 3.

Some people believe it's best to live with no regrets. I'm not sure if that's even possible. Even if it were, to do so would be to miss out on valuable information, new insight, countering points of view, and new ways of looking at old facts. "If only this, then that" kind of thinking is actually good for you. At least it can be, if you use it to your advantage rather than marinating in it to the point where you feel stewed in overwhelm.

The truth is we gain meaning and are propelled into action by identifying and naming the alternative choices we've made that may not have turned out like we planned. To deny regret is to miss a chance for growth and to make a better choice next time.

When it comes to regret, there are two main ways of reacting to a problem.

1. Change the situation
2. Change your mind

When we opt for changing the situation, we take steps to create a better outcome: We go back to school, we build a network, we reach out to people, we research, we apply for jobs, and we start our own business, and so on. We also act quickly.

When we decide to reframe it and change our minds, we rework the situation in our minds so that it no longer seems as bad.

Since I know for certain that clarity will not come from thinking alone, the purpose of this chapter is to help you identify the regrets that may be holding you back, look deeper into how you describe them to yourself, and act quickly to change the situation.

From Fear to Architect: Changing the Situation

My friend Scott took a big risk when he decided to make a career change. In his early twenties Scott graduated from college with a degree in engineering, and then worked in a variety of different jobs in his field. He had a great time traveling the world as a very well paid engineer, developing cool technology and working with really smart people; however, all he really wanted to do was be an architect and do his own thing. Architecture offered him the problem solving and critical thinking aspects of engineering with a more inspired, artistic aspect of idea development, which he loved.

Scott dreamed about it and talked to people about it, but every time he talked to architects they told him how impossible the field is to succeed in. They told him how long it would take him to go from grunt worker to practicing architect, let alone successful owner of his own firm, and that the road was thankless, exhausting, and lacked significant monetary rewards, considering all of the work it required of them.

For seven years he listened to that. For seven years he told himself his dream wasn't going to happen. For seven years he told himself that he could not afford it, he and his wife couldn't survive without his income, and they'd never recover if he pursued it. And for seven years all he could think about was becoming an architect and how much he regretted listening to the naysayers instead of himself.

One day, after imagining himself doing the work he was doing for the rest of his life, Scott decided that he didn't care what the "experts" said and that if he didn't go after what he wanted he would regret it for the rest of his life. He decided to change his situation.

He attended an Ivy League architecture school. He graduated, worked at the school for a couple of years after graduation, and recently he was offered a job at a dream firm doing the work he has always imagined. He and his wife live in a tiny apartment in New York City, he gets excited when he comes home to Boulder, Colorado, because he can get a good shot of tequila for only $20, and if you ask him about his work, his entire face will light up like the Fourth of July.

I have heard a hundred stories like this in researching this topic. The stories of "I can't do this because ..." have common threads, which are paralyzing and uninspiring. The magic happens when, for whatever reason, a person realizes the regret is too big to bear and that the story about why she can't change her situation is old and stale and doesn't work for her anymore. She decides that she wants the dream career more than she wants to live with the regret that will only be diluted by harnessing the power of it to get into action.

From Career Hopper to Portfolio Career Designer: Changing Your Mind

I was stuck for a long time in my business. I had set myself up to be unhappy in my work by designing a business that required me to do work I didn't like and I couldn't see a way out. I was so convinced that I couldn't do what I wanted and make money that I kept buying into the story and putting my career switch on hold. All the while I was regretting my choices and digging myself deeper into a hole. I wasn't able to break out of that business until I changed my mind about what was possible for me. Once I did that, however, the shift was so dramatic and I had so much clarity about what actions I wanted to take that I saw everything in a new light.

After I made that switch, I wrote this book, a book I had started seven years earlier, I began working with interesting clients, I began investigating in earnest how to move forward with other sides of my career and I shook the dust off of a copywriting and freelance writing business that brings me an immeasurable amount of joy. I have reinvented myself again and I feel fresher and more excited about my work than I have in years. And when I did all of that and finally dropped into the work I cared about, I also discovered some other work I wanted to do that I never would have been open to if I had stayed in that business.

When I look back and try to figure out how I could have been so seduced by the money that I was willing to give everything I loved up, I think my desire for safety (money) and my desire to do interesting and purposeful work just kept duking it out and money kept winning.

Two beliefs had to rise to the top before I was going to allow my situation to change.

1. I had to reconnect with my values and my beliefs about doing crazy good work.
2. I had to believe that if I just stuck with the work I loved and focused on contributing the very best of who I am and the very best of my work to the fields in which I was most interested, that I could achieve the highest level with it. Safety would be a byproduct of that focus, not the driving force behind my actions.

Now that I am doing more of the work I care about people ask me if I regret all of the time I spent "off track."

For a while I did. I was frustrated and angry, and I would often say to myself, *Imagine how much further along you'd be if you had just stayed focused on what you wanted and not gone down the rabbit hole.* But that was wasteful energy, especially when I think about all of the good things that came from my detour.

•   I was immersed in the world of business and online marketing for five years, I helped clients double and triple their income, and learned so much that I can apply to the current iteration of my copywriting business and use to help my clients. Whether they want to start a business or need help creating a compelling online presence, I have a lot to offer. I love having problems to solve. When it comes to marketing ideas, I never seem to run out. My copywriting clients love that.

•   I made some fantastic friends in the online marketing space, created cool programs, spoke at interesting events, and hosted unique and game changing retreats for women entrepreneurs. In fact, some of my dearest friends in the world right now are the ones I made while doing that work.

When I think about what my life would be like without them I would take that detour again any day.

- Going through all of this has given me a surplus of tools I can share with my clients who are trying to reinvent themselves and their careers.

- I now have a tremendous amount of patience for people who feel stuck, people who want to make a change and can't see their way through. I always had the training and hundreds of hours working with clients who were trying to find their ideal career or place in the world to draw on; however, having now gone through a similar experience myself adds texture I would not have had otherwise. Changing careers is a big transition and a process that doesn't happen overnight. I am more equipped now than ever before to write about this topic.

Yes, while there is a price to pay for putting off doing the work you love, that cost can always be mitigated if you drop any regrets you have and just do what you can do today to act on your desires.

Changing my mind about the regrets I have had about my career path has taught me one of the most valuable lessons ever: The person we are changes all of the time. As long as we are still alive and kicking, it is never too late to change either our minds or our situations, and maybe both. I'm not sure who said this, otherwise I would give credit where credit is due, but I remember hearing in graduate school that five years is the rough time frame that includes the life of the current you. Meaning, when you spend time regretting decisions you made many years ago, you're attempting to access a person that really no longer exists. It's unproductive and it undercuts your ability to make the best choices you can in *this* moment. You aren't your past. That's a liberating thought to me, and hopefully it is for you, too.

WRITE THAT SH*T DOWN

The mental scripts we carry around with us often drive us to choose paths and make choices without our realizing it. In this exercise you're going to uncover some of the scripts that might be holding you back so you can move more quickly toward your ideal work.

Priming the Pump

It's possible that you have thoughts about what might have been had some action, detail, or outcome in the past been different. *What could have happened?* These are the wouldas and shouldas of your life. They are the "if only" thoughts that keep you glued to the past. They can either paralyze you or help create the momentum you need to move forward.

For this exercise, set your timer for five minutes and write down every "if only" that comes to mind when you reflect on the path your career has taken.

Example: "If only I had done *this* than *this* never would have happened."

Example: "I chose *blank* when I should have chosen *blank*."

Go.

Write a Letter to Regret

Now that you have made a list of all of the "if onlys" in your mind, you are ready to write a letter to Regret as it relates to the big career decision that is challenging you right now.

What do you need to let go of? How can you look deeper into the regret to see how there was more than one way the event in question happened? How might your situation have turned out worse if you had chosen the other path? How have you used comparisons to other people to allow the regret to grow? How could you reframe your regret, or what can you do right away, to show yourself that changing your situation is far more important to you than hanging on to your regret?

How will you know when you've truly let go of the regret?

Go.

Write a Letter to the Lessons

The great thing about regret is that within that emotion exists a backlog of lessons that we've likely learned without even being conscious about it. For this letter I want you to contemplate all of the perceived negative outcomes you've experienced throughout your career. Maybe you were fired once or demoted, maybe you really wanted a job but weren't offered the position, maybe you were offered the job but turned down the offer and then wished you hadn't. Write down everything that happened and then find the lesson and how you took that lesson into other areas of your life and you used it to your benefit. Here's a snippet from one of my client's letter to her Lessons.

When I didn't get that job that I wanted I took it so personally that I could barely get out of bed in the morning. I quit looking because I was convinced nobody was ever going to want me. The problem was that I became so emotionally tied to them saying no that I failed to see what a blessing it actually was. The truth was I wanted to win more than I wanted that particular job. When it came down to it that job was in direct conflict with some of the values I said were necessary in my life: weekends to spend with my family, and to travel, and the flexibility to be there for my sons during the week if an emergency came up. In truth I would not have had any of that. My ego had just been so destroyed that I couldn't see it. The greatest lesson I learned from that was that when it is time to look for work I have to take my ego out of it and remember to focus on the work I would be doing, how it lines up with my values, and the kind of lifestyle I want rather than being focused on "winning" the job hunt contest. I am glad I learned that lesson. It just took me a long time to be able to see it.

Play with It

Let's turn your every "If only" into a "Now I." Whatever regret you have, whatever "if only" statement has been holding you back, pretend that it no longer has the control. You do. Now is what matters. Use your regret as a springboard for further action.

Research your options, but don't get stuck there. Act quickly. Hurl yourself headfirst into the unknown and don't be so worried about getting it right that you stop yourself.

Concern yourself *only* with who you are today, in this moment and act from that place. If you do something and it turns out badly, then you'll still be better off. Not so if you leave a situation undone.

Make a plan for what you are going to do and then do it right away. The most successful people are those who kick themselves the hardest after they make mistakes and get over their intense regret faster than anyone else. After that, they take immediate action.

Wash. Rinse. Repeat.

After you complete your letters and before you begin the next chapter, be sure to head over to www.careerswitch.org/2review to get some more writing prompts and review what you've discovered so far.

Chapter 3
I Wrote a Letter to Indecision and My Values Wrote Me Back

Caterpillar: "And who are you?"Alice: "I...I hardly know, sir, just at present-at least I know who I was when I got up this morning, but I think must have changed several times since then."

- Lewis Carroll

One of my favorite exercises to do with clients is to ask them to describe exactly what they want from whatever area of their life is the most unsatisfying. It's fairly easy for them to list the details about what they want. In fact, the clarity is often surprising to me, especially when I take it one step further. Once they tell me what they want, I ask them to write down every action they've taken in the previous week on behalf of their goal. Inevitably, when they are unsatisfied with that area of their work and life, what they spent their time on did not line up with what they said they wanted. Is this just a matter of them lying to me, or maybe lying to themselves? Not necessarily. What's usually happening is that they are unsure of what they value most. However, watch how someone spends their week and you will be able to make a relatively good guess about what they value most.

The best part about getting clear on your values is that when you do decisions become much easier. In fact, they become so easy that you just begin to act more in line with them without even realizing you're making a conscious decision to do so.

When I was working as a marketing consultant there were many times when my values and my clients' values didn't match up. When that happened, continuing to work with them became a daily challenge. I often justified my decision to stay by telling myself that it was normal to not always see eye to eye with my clients, that I didn't have the luxury of quitting just because I didn't agree with my clients, and that the money was too good to give up.

The problem was that no matter how many times I tried to ignore it or pretend that the good outweighed the bad, being involved in work that was in conflict with what I valued became a cancer in my life. I felt its heavy undercurrent, I felt bad about myself and even worse, I felt ashamed for choosing money above all else. What made it especially challenging was that the money was good enough that it allowed me to live in accordance with some of my other top values such as freedom, time with my family, and time for learning and inquiry; so, I let it go on much longer than I should.

The breakthrough I experienced that allowed me to walk away from doing work that was against my values was when I finally clarified what mine actually were. I thought I knew what they were, but my ignorance was evident by how incongruent I felt. When adding that experience to all of the work I have done with clients I am convinced that clarifying your own values is one of the most important steps you can take on your path to achieving career clarity.

WRITE THAT SH*T DOWN

Now you're going to spend some time clarifying your values.

Priming the Pump

Here's a simple process you can follow to identify your values:

1. Make a list of your values. You can find a comprehensive list of values at Careerswitch.org/valuelist.
2. Rank your values from most important to least important.

3. Once you have your list, take each value and give an example of how you lived in accordance with that value recently, preferably in the past week. For example, a potential client contacted me a couple of weeks ago to write some copy for him. He was willing to pay me well for my services but I just didn't feel good about the project. I felt the "no" strongly in my gut and therefore I referred him to someone else.

4. Next, take each value and give an example of how you did not live in accordance with your value. How did it make you feel? What did you say to yourself to make it okay to go against your values? Did you realize it in the moment or is it only something you are able to see in hindsight? What's an important lesson you can learn from choosing to behave in a manner incongruent with your values?

When it comes to your career, ideally you will choose to do work where acting on behalf of your top values is easy. It is rare for this always to be the case, especially when you're working for a large company. If your top values are not mirrored by your company's top values, at the very least you should stay clear of doing work that goes *against* your values.

When you match up your work with your values you feel at peace, decisions become easy, opportunities present themselves, and you are free to do the kind of work that makes you feel good at the end of the day.

Write a Letter to Your Values

For this letter, take your top five values and write a letter to them. Tell them why they are important to you and the kind of person you get to be when you live your life in alignment with these values.

Play with It

This one is easy. Whenever you're faced with a decision at work or whenever you're considering different career options, use your values as a filter. Think about what you'll be doing in your work, what you're expected to believe and promote, and then make sure there's a match. It's a simple process but one that makes decision making a breeze.

After you complete your letters and before you begin the next chapter, be sure to head over to www.careerswitch.org/3review to get some more writing prompts and review what you've discovered so far.

Chapter 4
I Wrote a Letter to My What and How, and the Way Wrote Me Back

"You have to leave the city of your comfort and go into the wilderness of your intuition. What you'll discover will be wonderful. What you'll discover is yourself."

—Alan Alda

One of my all time favorite questions to ask clients who come to me hoping to answer the question of what to do next is: "What can you not help but be?"

Most of the time when I say that, they pause for a moment, I suspect because they are waiting for me to complete the question. But, that's it. *What can you not help but be?*

When posed this question many people stumble at first and when the answer comes, it's usually expressed triumphantly. "Yes, of course, I am a _____!"

We are many things and certainly there is no single word that can define who we are (which is why I asked *what* are you and not *who* are you) but at our core we all embody certain traits, qualities, temperaments, and characteristics of which some are more prominent than others. This is not an effort to limit you or reduce you to one way of being. Rather, it is just one step in achieving a deeper level clarity on what you want for your career.

Now it's my turn to ask you the question: What can you not help but be? In case you need words to get you started, here's a list. Feel free to add your own words to this list if none of these does a good job of describing you.

- Activist

- Advocate

- Builder

- Caretaker

- Communicator

- Connector

- Developer

- Entertainer

- Facilitator

- Fixer

- Innovator

- Intellectual

- Inventor

- Judger

- Leader

- Learner

- Nurturer

- Optimizer

- Organizer

- Socializer

- Teacher

Once you have your word, write it down, paint it, mold it out of clay, or do anything else you can imagine so that you can see it in front of you. You can even make it big while you're at it. Put it some place you can see it and write down the feelings you're experiencing as you look at it.

Does it feel like it represents you? Do you feel good connecting to that word or does it feel restricting?

When I was studying to be a counselor, we once did an exercise where we were told to write down ten adjectives that described us . . . and that also resonated with us or made us feel good. Then we had to order them from what we thought described us best to what we thought describes us the least. These were fun little exercises until our professor told us that we had to pare down our list to only five adjectives.

This seems like a very simple exercise, I realize. However, something rather surprising happened. When we had to give up our adjectives a lot of people in the room felt like they were truly giving them up. Meaning, once they were no longer on their list, then somehow they could no longer be described that way.

Obviously that's not a rational thought. We all knew better than to think just because it was not written down in front of us that we were no longer allowed to be described in that way, but for some reason we still felt it.

When I've had people do the exercise I am walking you through here, where you choose one word that most accurately defines what you are, some have become very uneasy with the idea of picking just one. They see themselves as five slices of greatness and the idea of not getting to include the other four makes them anxious. Not to worry. There's a reason you pick just one and that will become clear as we move forward.

The How

The next question I have for you is this: How do you want to do what you are?

Start by putting the word you just chose at the top of your mind and then think about how you would like to *do* that thing you can't help being.

Here are a few examples taken from others who have done this exercise:

- "I am an intellectual and the way I most enjoy embodying this quality is by doing research."

- "I am a leader and the way I most enjoy leading is by managing teams of people."

- "I am a teacher and the way I most enjoy teaching is through writing." (That one's mine!)

Now it's your turn.

How do you want to do what you are? What is the easiest, most enjoyable and satisfying way you express yourself as an innovator (or an activist or a fixer or a builder)?

Write that down now just like I did in the examples I shared above. How does that feel?

When I connected the teacher and the writing for me it felt natural and comfortable and easy. And even though I knew that was only one part of my career picture, I also was excited by the thought of it. However, that excitement paled in comparison to how I felt after I completed the trifecta, which is what you're going to do next.

The Way

Now that you have your "what" and your "how," you are going to dive into the "way." I'm going to show you how this works by using an example from someone who said he could not help but be a teacher. He was a middle school teacher, which is one reason his strong desire for a career change was causing him so much confusion. He knew at heart that he was a teacher but he was really unsatisfied in the role he had been playing as one. This exercise cleared it up for him.

Brett was a teacher, and he said that the way he liked to express that part of him was by sharing his expertise on the topics he was passionate about with people who were excited to learn. Notice he did not say anything about being in a room with kids all day. His key phrases were "share expertise," "topics he was passionate about," and "people excited to learn." He might have been getting two out of the three in the classroom, though probably *only* two. There certainly were other places he could get all three.

Once he identified those three critical indicators, I had him make a list of every job he could possibly think of that would allow him to teach where all three requirements would be met.

Here's a part of that list:

- Peace Corps volunteer
- Trainer
- Tour guide (travel)
- Experiential education leader
- Wilderness instructor
- Cycling guide
- Relief worker
- Expedition guide
- Forest ranger
- Docent
- Outward Bound or Nolls instructor
- Camp owner and director

Brett had trained to be a teacher and had spent ten-plus years in the classroom, but he felt stuck. Still, he didn't see himself in corporate America, and being an entrepreneur didn't interest him either. Even though each spring when his contract came up for renewal he wanted finally to choose not to sign, he couldn't see a way past his dilemma. He was also confused because he felt in his heart of hearts that he was supposed to be a teacher, but nothing about teaching in a school setting excited him anymore. Once Brett started creating a list of jobs that represented other ways of being a teacher he was able to make a plan to do something about it. He finally became confident that when the next spring came around he wouldn't be signing anything except his letter of resignation.

In the end, Brett designed a portfolio career in which he does several of the jobs that he originally listed. He never thought he'd be drawn to such variety (and often some instability) but he came to realize that as long as he got to share his expertise about topics he was passionate about with people who were excited to learn, he could stay in his groove and that's all that mattered.

WRITE THAT SH*T DOWN

Now it's time for you to discover how to bring together your "what", your "how" and your "way".

Priming the Pump

Take your "what" and your "how" and write them at the top of a blank page like this:

> *"I am a _____ and how I most enjoy expressing that is by or through _____. Here's a list of specific jobs that would allow me to do that."*

Then, make a list, like Brett did, of all of the jobs you have ever heard about that might match your requirements. Do some research, go online, talk to people you know who've done similar work. See if you can come up with at least twenty possibilities.

Next, read through the list. Circle the ones that make you thoroughly giddy when you imagine yourself getting to do them.

Finally, pick the one you are most excited about. That's the career prospect to which you're going to write a letter.

Write a Letter to Your Way

For this letter, take the "job" you chose in the priming the pump exercise and tell it why you get so excited when you imagine yourself doing it for a living. What sounds interesting, challenging, and fun about it? How does it align with your values? What do you believe would get to happen for you if you found a way to do it? What do you see are the greatest challenges to making it happen? Who can you talk to, to learn more or get the support you need?

Keep this job in mind as we'll be referring back to it again in Chapter 6.

Play with It

The only actions you need to take for this are to:

- Add to your list of possible jobs, roles, or businesses, and
- Reach out to people who might be able to offer you more information about the day-to-day realities of those jobs.

This experience and information will help you a lot as we move further along in the process.

After you complete your letters and before you begin the next chapter, be sure to head over to www.careerswitch.org/4review to get some more writing prompts and review what you've discovered so far.

Chapter 5
I Wrote a Letter to
My Greatness and It Told Me to
Get My Butt in Gear

"Always be a first rate version of yourself and not a second rate version of someone else."

—Judy Garland

"Are you willing to be great?"

That's what one of my writing mentors asked me once when I told her what I wanted to do with my career.

"Yes," I said without hesitation.

"No," she said. "I mean, are you truly willing to be really great?"

Again, I thought my answer was yes, but I pressed for more. I said, "What I really want is to live an interesting life, to be interesting, to be interested, to do work that is worth writing about and then write about it until my hand hurts. I'm willing to do whatever it takes to do that."

"Great," she said. "In order to do that, you have to first be willing to be really great."

Starting to think I was being dense, I said, "Okay then. What does that mean? How will I know if I am being really great?"

Here's the list she gave me. To be really great you have to:

• Work every single day at being great at whatever you choose to do.

- Do it because not doing it is not an option. It can't just be something you kind of want to do. "Kind of like" won't get you to greatness.

- Put in long hours even when you don't want to. Especially when you don't want to.

- Figure out how to make money doing something else until you figure out how to make money doing work you truly care about.

- Not care when people talk shit about you. You can't get taken out when people tell you that you suck or that your ideas are stupid. You can't let what other people say take you off track.

At the end of the conversation she added, *"And, no matter what it comes from, your greatness had better add value to other people."*

When I hung up the phone with my mentor, I was equal parts revived and defeated. I wanted to be great. I wanted to be the kind of person who could be really great and whose greatness could impact other people in a positive way. I also heard the whispers that told me that even if I did everything she said, I still wouldn't be great. So why try?

I listened to those whispers of doubt for a long time.

I'm not sure what I was waiting for. Maybe I was waiting for someone to come down and crown me worthy enough to try being great. Or maybe I wanted someone to tell me before I even got started that I never would be great enough. That would have surely let me off the hook.

The idea of greatness intrigued me. On some level it seemed like greatness was reserved for the special few. I had seen greatness for sure, but I had definitely seen much more okayness than I had seen greatness, so if the word could be thrown around like it was possible for anyone, then why hadn't more people achieved real greatness? Why did it seem that most people were okay with just doing fine?

That conversation took place several years ago. Afterwards, during my period of waiting for greatness to land on my doorstep, I became a voracious reader about anything and everything having to do with aptitudes, talent, and practice. I talked to people, read books and academic journals, and studied the role of deliberate practice in expert performance. Basically, I decided to put off my own greatness so I could study the greatness of others.

My questions were:

- What makes those who are truly great different from the rest of us?
- Is greatness achievable by everyone? If it is, why are there so few who are really great and so many who are only doing just fine?
- How do we become expert at something as adults? Is it possible to bloom late and bloom big? (I believe that part of being great involves being a master of something.)
- Does our ability to become an expert at something have more to do with our interests or our aptitudes?
- Is there such a thing as talent?
- Where does practice fit in?
- Have some people been given extra gifts?

Heading into my research on the topic of greatness, I was hoping the answer was that to be an expert at something you have to have an intense interest in it, and then you have to practice it like your life depended on it, though not necessarily for 10,000 hours as Malcolm Gladwell claims in his book *The Outliers*.[1] Primarily I was hoping to find some case studies of people who found work or hobbies later in life and subsequently became truly great from practice. At forty-one years old with a six-year old daughter to care for my days of being able to practice any one thing for ten hours a day were over. I wanted to know that it was never too late to become truly great at something new despite what some research might be suggesting.

Part of me was also hoping that what all of the research would really bear out was that we can only go as far as our talents allow: that some people have been given extra gifts and some haven't. That seemed unlikely, however, and frankly, it would let us off the hook way too easily if it were true.

In the end, I discovered that greatness comes at the intersection of interest, aptitude, practice, commitment, and belief.

Interests and Aptitudes

By the time I was the most unhappy I've ever been in my career, I had probably taken one hundred career interest and personality tests. I knew my codes, my types, my temperaments, and my interests. Obviously you have to have an interest in something to do it well, but that's not enough to build a career or a business on. You have to have an interest and also an aptitude for it if you want to achieve the highest level with it. Although I knew what my interests were, what I didn't know was what to do with the pages of possible career choices all of those results about my interests afforded me.

Sure, I could have picked one that was the most interesting and see what happened, but that felt like a waste of time. Besides, the last time that happened I ended up in the absolutely wrong place. I wound up driving home from my volunteer shift in the emergency room wondering, "Why is this not the match my type said it would be?" (By "not the match," I mean the absolute most off-the-mark match possible). I was certain there had to be a way to find out what I was actually good at rather than simply what sounded interesting to me and what might have been a fit for my personality.

The next day, I called up the Johnson O'Conner Research Foundation in Denver, Colorado, and made my appointment.[2] The Foundation's mission is to help people discover their natural potential by identifying their personal strengths so they can apply them to their careers.

After two full days and twenty-two different tests, here are the kinds of work that were suggested by my aptitude pattern.

- Journalist/writer
- Teaching and researching
- Consulting
- Mediation
- Advertising, marketing, and public relations

- Small business owner (and I should specialize, so that I am an expert on something specific)

Oddly enough, or maybe obviously enough, for the twenty-five years prior to taking that test I had been writing and teaching. During the immediate five years leading up to the test, I was doing those two activities as well as consulting on marketing as part of owning my own business. Five out of the six activities I had been doing were the exact five behaviors that reflected my highest aptitudes. The sixth one, mediation, was actually one that was always in the back of my mind and the one I had been gravitating toward for the past five years. Seeing marketing on that list surprised me because I hated doing it so much; however, just because we have an aptitude for something, it doesn't always mean we're going to like doing it.

In hindsight, I think all I wanted to get from the testing was permission or a pat on the back telling me I was already in the right place. This test also made me understand why so many fields I had an interest in and had tried in the past actually turned out to be a huge challenge for me. I didn't have the aptitude for them so it was like I was always swimming upstream. It was a relief to finally let those career options go for good.

Even though my aptitudes reflected work I was already doing and I felt sure I was at least in the right neighborhood with my career, I couldn't escape the thought that if I had actually been doing one of the activities that came naturally to me for my whole life, writing, why had I yet to achieve greatness as a writer? I had the interest and the ability, I had definitely put in the hours, and I had the support, so what was I missing?

It turns out I was missing three critical elements.

1. A plan that included intense deliberate practice.
2. A specific direction for my writing.
3. The belief that if I put in the work, deliberately, day after day and year after year, there was at least a chance I could achieve great performance.

During that testing experience I learned that my abilities or desires were not what were constraining me. It was my beliefs.

I learned a lot from that experience, and as soon as I arrived home I told my friends all about the testing. Actually, I wrote about it, hoping that one of them would be interested enough to do it themselves. One of them did and afterwards, I sat down with Julie so she could tell me about her experience.

Julie (JulieSimth.com) is a family educator and counselor who helps parents connect with their teens and "tweens" (kids between the ages of nine and twelve). She decided to take the aptitude test because she was in the middle of a difficult divorce, felt like she was at a fork in the road regarding her work, and she was looking for permission to do what she wanted to do. Like many career changers, she was looking for the green light to do the work that was in her heart, any indication that would let her know the risk was worth it; and there was a better shot than not that she would be able to pull it off successfully.

She told me that what surprised her most about the testing was how frustrated she'd become by the tests that were difficult and how quickly she'd discounted the activities that were easy. It was as though what was easy wasn't valuable enough. She also said that this had been a pattern in her life for as long as she could remember: She often pushed herself to do what she couldn't do, or what presented the greatest difficulty, because she believed there was something wrong with her if she couldn't do all things well. She has now realized how much that faulty thinking was holding her back.

She told me she felt immediately lighter the moment she even considered focusing on what came naturally to her. She had decided at last that she was going to be able to give up splitting her energies among too many activities as well as those that didn't serve her and focus on doing just a few that lit her heart and mind on fire.

Julie admitted that she walked into the O'Conner Research Foundation offices hoping for a magic pill—the one answer that would guide her to the single best career path—but left with something far better: deeper perspective, permission excitement about being herself – her true self.

I am not a trainer or an affiliate of the Johnson O'Connor Research Foundation, and I do not receive any type of compensation for referring people to them, but it's the one thing that I recommend my clients do. Testing is not cheap, but the information you get about yourself when you take the tests is invaluable when it comes to career reinvention. It opens you up to a whole new way of thinking about how to use your skills. Even if you're confident that you know your top skills, there is something empowering about actually watching yourself take the tests. Whether you're trying to construct wiggly blocks, remember Martian words, perform fine motor activities, or identify tones, you'll learn information about yourself that you'd miss by only taking a paper and pencil test.

Practice

In his book *Talent Is Overrated* (Portfolio Trade, 2010), Geoffrey Colvin says, "Deliberate practice is hard. It hurts. But it works. More of it equals better performance. Tons of it equals great performance."[3] I would agree, and I would add to this thought that, as far as I am concerned, it is worth it. I am interested in being a master of my craft.

If you're reading this book, my guess is that doing something competently is not going to be enough for you. You, like me, want to be an expert, to master something, to drop into the kind of work that will let you grow and climb the kind of ladder that never ends. If you want to be an expert, practice and time will help get you there.

If you've ever read any of Benjamin Franklin's letters you know why they are held in such esteem. He wrote something on the order of 198 letters, just those we know about, and he is considered one of the most prolific and influential writers in history. However, what's truly remarkable about his writing was his process.

In *Talent Is Overrated*, Colvin describes Franklin's efforts to become a better writer. Apparently, one day when Ben was young, his father came across a series of letters he had been exchanging with a friend concerning the topic of education. Ben thought women should be educated and his friend did not. His father told Ben what was good about his letters (mainly spelling and punctuation), and then he showed him where he was falling short compared to his friend. He said, "In elegance of expression, in method and in perspicuity, of which he convinced me by several instances."[4]

Instead of giving up or accepting his current efforts as his best, Franklin set off on an arduous journey to improve his writing that most of us would never consider. One of the habits he cultivated was searching for examples of writing that was far superior to anything he had ever come close to producing. He took the English periodical *The Spectacle* and began dissecting the articles in it. First he would read an article and make notes on the meaning of each sentence. Next, a few days later, he would return to his notes and attempt to express the meaning of each sentence in his own words. Finally, he would compare his version to the original essay, find the flaws, and then work to correct them.

One of the first weaknesses he realized was that he was lacking an abundant vocabulary. In order to remedy the situation, he decided to rewrite *The Spectator* essays in verse. He would walk away from his poems for a few days and when he returned to them he would rewrite them in prose, once again always comparing his essays to the originals.

When he noticed that he struggled with organization he came up with an idea where he would make short notes about each sentence from an essay and write each note on a separate sheet of paper. He would then walk away from the essay for a few weeks, until he had forgotten all about its structure and content, and when he returned to it he would mix up all of the slips of paper and attempt to put all of the notes back in the right order and rewrite the essay. Naturally he would then compare his to the original.

The amazing thing about this is that he did all of this on his own. No prompting from a teacher or a boss was required. He chose a target, writing that in his mind represented the best available to him in prose, and he created a structured and deliberate practice so that he would see consistent improvement in his own writing.

We often talk about practicing the skills we want to get better at, but many of us have not learned the art of deliberate practice. Or maybe we knew what it was like as kids, but we've let it go. Many essay writers who want to become better essay writers try and write more essays, but that's not necessarily practice. It's just more writing.

Deliberate practice requires practicing something that is the most challenging. It involves a commitment to specific and sustained efforts to do something you can't do well. Tennis champion Roger Federer, ranked first in the world at the time of this writing, is evidence of this principle. He did not become the tennis player he is because he spent hours hitting balls that were fed to him. He's the best because he spent hours on end playing in the wind, hitting shots on the run, racing to get nearly un-gettable drop shots, and playing for six hours at a stretch in hot and humid weather to make sure he was ready for those long five set standoffs against his opponent on Centre Court at Wimbledon, and concentrating in a manner that would baffle most. Playing eight hours of tennis a day is not enough. Playing four hours a day of the hardest tennis you will ever see might be.

The famous violinist Nathan Milstein wrote: "Practice as much as you feel you can accomplish with concentration. Once when I became concerned because others around me practiced all day long, I asked [my mentor] Professor Auer how many hours I should practice, and he said, 'It really doesn't matter how long. If you practice with your fingers, no amount is enough. If you practice with your head, two hours is plenty.'"[5]

In a *Psychological Review* article, psychologists K. Anders Ericsson, Ralf T. Krampe, and Clemens Tesch-Römer argue, "Expert performance is qualitatively different from normal performance and even that expert performers have characteristics and abilities that are qualitatively different from or at least outside the range of those of normal adults. However, we deny that these differences are immutable, that is, due to innate talent. Only a few exceptions, most notably height, are genetically prescribed. Instead, we argue that the differences between expert performers and normal adults reflect a life-long period of deliberate effort to improve performance in a specific domain."[6]

This is the same information described by Geoffrey Colvin and also by journalist Malcolm Gladwell in his book on the nature of success, *The Outliers* (Little, Brown and Company, 2008). Both authors have asserted in their books that it's the deliberate practice over thousands of hours that sets expert performers apart. That's good news and bad news. Bad news because as we get older practicing thousands of hours on any one thing is a significant challenge. Good news because even though we might have less time to practice than a teenager trying to make the Olympic team, practice is something within our control and we can get very good at making each second count. The trick then is in knowing what you want to practice—and, the *knowing* has to be honest and come from deep within. This is where commitment comes in.

Commitment

Unless you really know you want to develop an ability or master something in your career and you're willing to do whatever it takes to attain it, then your commitment will falter and you'll be willing to risk less. That's why many projects die on the vine, why applications don't get sent in, why careers never change, why the final chapters of books are seldom written, and why some people spend their days wishing "If only . . . ."

What does it mean to truly commit to something? Successful performance whether in sports, career, or life depends on your ability to be fully committed to your goals for an extended period of time. When you commit to something you are saying that the other competing interests that will show up in your life on a daily basis will not take you away from acting on behalf of your primary goal. This is common sense. You know this already. However, when it comes to career change this is what separates those who make the change success-fully and those who decide to stay with what's comfortable. We'll talk about this more in the next chapter.

One of the best ways to remain committed to your outcome is to gather sup-port from others. According to psychological educator Benjamin S. Bloom's research, detailed in his book *Developing Talent in Young People* (Ballantine Books, 1985), there are three common denominators that are true of all expert performers: They practice intensively and deliberately, they study with devoted teachers, and they are supported enthusiastically by their families throughout their developing years.[7] Unconditional support is not always easy to find as adults. When we were kids it was a lot easier. We had teachers and parents and coaches who constantly supported the love we had for something and made it easy for us to do it. They helped us set up our lives so we could do more of it. As adults, most people don't care or even notice if we don't get our ass in gear and do what we love. In fact, a lot of times we are told to let go of what we love because we have real life and real bills staring us in the face. When you can find people who will truly support your efforts, then you can make anything happen. One of the best gifts we can get from others while we are in the middle of a big change is borrowed belief, which we'll talk about next.

Belief

No matter how much you love something, how much you practice, how good you are and how committed you are, you won't achieve greatness if you don't believe you're already great enough to achieve it. It's not always easy however to tap into that greatness when you're struggling to find your way. When I am in a place like that I sometimes have to borrow the belief that others have in me to keep going until I can tap into it myself.

I remember one time in particular when I was desperately struggling to find my way as a writer. I was attending a retreat hosted by one of my mentors, Jennifer Louden, and while we were sitting across from each other on the grounds of the Mabel Dodge Luhan House in Taos, Jen sat back patiently as I rattled on about all of my doubts and stories and God knows what. When I was finished and catching my breath she looked at me and said, "Melani, you are a writer." I wasn't yet at the place where I believed it; however, because there was a part of me that felt it was true, I was able to use her belief in me until I was able to catch up.

You have to believe you have the gifts to make something happen and that there's no limit to how far you can go. If you don't have the belief yet, borrow it and then get busy sharing your gifts. Which reminds me, this might be a good time to let you know about the five gifts you may not even know you have.

Gift 1: Your Why

Even though you may struggle to define your "why," (the reason you do what you do and make the choices you make) I'm betting you know what it is.

Sometimes we avoid asking ourselves what our "why" is because it seems big and we're afraid if we no longer hide the truth from ourselves that we'll have no other choice but to act on it.

Sometimes people will avoid their "why" by asking the wrong question when it comes to a career choice. They will ask themselves, "What do I want to do?" But that's not the question that will lead to the information that really matters. That's the easy and safe question. You get to your crazy good "why" by asking these questions:

- What do I want more of in my life?
- What do I want less of?
- Why am I doing this? Why do I want to career switch?
- What do I hope to gain from this change?
- What kind of day, week, month, year am I hoping this change affords me?
- Who am I hoping to impact or serve from this change?

I suspect that when you answer these questions your "why" will flow to the top really quickly. And let me tell you that your "why" is one of the greatest gifts you have. Your "why," if you have the courage to stay connected to it, is what will allow you to be great even when it would be easier to be good. Being clear on your "why" is what will keep you moving forward so that not only do you benefit from your progress but so will everyone you touch. Which brings us to your second gift.

Gift 2: Your Desire to Make a Contribution

You would not be reading this book or writing these letters if there was not a part of you that has a strong desire to contribute the best of who you are so others can benefit. Most of us are driven at some level to make a contribution to something greater than ourselves. We want to matter. We want our work to matter. It's one of our most basic psychological needs. When we know that we are contributing to a purpose that is greater than our own efforts we will be happy, productive, and driven to do more. When we embrace this gift, our desire to contribute, we will not allow ourselves to remain in work that leaves us empty. We will *do* whatever it takes to do more.

Gift 3: Your Inspiration to Make a Difference

If you are anything like me you're inspired by people who take their talents and use them to make a difference in the lives of others. I'm inspired by Kurtis Glade, a father of a child with Cystic Fibrosis who was laid off from his advertising job and decided to make a documentary about a surf camp that gives free lessons to kids with Cystic Fibrosis (http://www.kurtisglade.com/pages/mauli-ola-foundation). I'm inspired by Oral Lee Brown, the woman who sent a classroom of first graders to college. I'm inspired by Special Spaces, an organization that works to create dream rooms for children with life-threatening diseases. Maybe you're inspired by people who write beautiful poems, take spectacular photographs, or teach children. The fact is, you are inspired just as you have the ability to inspire.

You are not on the planet to merely use its resources and then be forgotten. You are here to make a difference to someone, maybe one someone, maybe hundreds of thousands of someones. It doesn't matter how many, what matters is that you do your work, that you don't waste the best of you and that you leave it all on the table. You have the potential to make a difference but you aren't going to give yourself the chance to do it if you stay somewhere that keeps you down or makes you question yourself. Your ability to make a difference is a gift you have. Don't let it go to waste because you are scared or unsure. We all are. That can't be reason enough to stop you from showing us your greatness.

Gift 4: Your Ability to Do Whatever You Can Imagine

One of my favorite quotes of all time is . . . *"Your imagination is your preview to life's coming attractions."* Albert Einstein said that and I agree with him.

Your ability to do anything you can imagine may be the greatest gift you have, for you can't imagine doing something without also the ability to do it on some level also being present at the same time. There are a thousand quotes I could share about this but all that needs to happen for you to use this gift that you already have is to not stop yourself. If you want something and you can see it clearly in your mind's eye, then you can make it happen. And you owe it to all of us to do it. If you envision something and don't act on it, you are allowing your gift to be latent. That's a waste none of us can afford.

You have the gift, so use it. One of the ways you can do that is by writing the letters in this book. Be specific, imagine phenomenal success and satisfaction for yourself and know that you can make whatever you want to happen happen.

Gift 5: Your Default to Succeed

Did you know that you are springloaded for success? Success is not a concept easily defined, as there are as many definitions as there are people. However, what is true for everyone is that success is a function of doing what you are designed to do and doing it with every ounce of energy and passion you have. That's the position you're set to, it's where your heart and mind wants you to be and it's where you will find the deepest level of satisfaction. Because your default is for success, we all win. True success, the kind of success that is based not solely on monetary gain or materials and toys, but on what makes us feel good from head to toe, is a contagious bug that has no vaccine. Spread it to the masses, leave no one out, and see what your greatness does for others.

These are the gifts you need to get where you want to go and the great thing is, you already have them. Whether they've been gathering a bit of dust or you need to fish them out of an old box in the attic, they're yours to do with as you see fit. When you combine these gifts with your interest, aptitudes, practice, and commitment, you'll be unstoppable.

WRITE THAT SH*T DOWN

In the writing exercises that follow you'll get the chance to connect with your greatness and consider new ways to access it.

Priming the Pump

In this written exercise, you are going to answer several questions. Give yourself five minutes to answer each question (some have multiple parts), with a minute or two between each for rest.

- When you are most like yourself what are you doing and experiencing? How are you contributing or being useful?

- What do you want to be known for? What are the contributions or impact you'd like to make?

- What are the activities you do that come most naturally to you? How do you think? How do you process information? Do you move quickly through projects or do you take your time? Are you an ideas person or do you love the details? How have these tendencies played out for you or against you in your work?

- What do you believe about what you can do? Do you think you have a choice? Do you believe that if you do the work of your dreams you can achieve the highest level with it?

- What are you willing to give up in order to get what you want?

Write a Letter to Your Greatness

This is one of the most difficult letters I have ever written. I remember staring at the blank page forever, trying to get an image in my head of me being the great self I wanted to be in my work. I ran the conversation with my mentor in my head a thousand times over, hearing her saying, "Are you truly ready to be really great?" It felt so immense and out of reach. I wondered if I really wanted to make the heavy investment with my writing that it takes to achieve greatness. I thought about the price I was willing, or not willing, to pay. I wondered how my answers would impact the people I loved most in my life.

Then I started and I couldn't stop. My letter surprised me. What I thought I was going to write was not what I ended up writing. This letter was a big turning point in my clarity seeking process. When I put it all out on paper, the message I received back was loud and clear: "Get your ass in gear sister. You've got work to do!"

When you write a letter to your greatness, first consider your five gifts and tell your greatness what they are. Tell it your "why," how you want to contribute, how your contributions will make a difference and to whom, what you imagine your work will be, what it will look like, and why you believe you can make it all happen. Then reflect back to what you wrote in the Priming the Pump exercise above. What do you want to be known for? What are the qualities you possess or the activities you do that come easy to you? What do you love that you're also great at doing? What do you want? What are you willing to give up and commit to in order to make it happen.

Then, talk to the part inside of you that needs to step up to make it all happen. Tell her what you need and want from her. Tell her what has to happen for you to be able to pull this off, day in and day out, no matter where and no matter what. Be as specific as you can. Drill it down to the big decisions and the small decisions you'll need to make each day regarding how you will spend your time. When you write this letter you should be blown away by not only the truth you'll learn about yourself, which *will* come out in this letter, but by what you envision for yourself. It will be big. It may even scare you. That's good because what that fear is telling you is that you're on the exact right track and once you step into this and you allow yourself to believe it can happen for you, you will have no choice but to throw all you have into it. It will be magnificent.

Play with It

This part is simple. You can't do this alone. Nobody who ever reached true greatness at anything ever has or ever will. Go find a mentor or a coach or a spectacular teacher. This should be someone who is not just a coach who is going to tell you *how* you can do something. This is someone who is actually *doing* what you want to do. Someone who is using the skills you want to be using on a daily basis, who has been doing it for a while and is successful. This person also has to be interested in investing time in you. He or she has to have a little skin in the game and be excited about seeing you grow in your field and as a person.

I found my mentor by looking for people who were building the kind of business I wanted in a way that resonated for me, and who were making money doing it. I reached out to her for some coaching, after watching what she was doing and how she was growing for a long time, to see if I liked her as much in a one-on-one conversation as I did in her writing. I told her what I wanted to do with my work. She challenged me, asked questions, and once I passed the "test" we were off and running. It was one of the best phone calls I've ever made.

Tell your mentor exactly what you want to do, lay out your dream no matter how big or silly it may sound and let him or her know exactly what you plan on doing to make it happen. If you can get someone on your side who believes in you then you will not only shave time and effort off the change process but you'll learn lessons you will take with you for the rest of your life. There's nothing like knowing someone is rooting for you and is in your corner when you're faced with challenges along the way. And remember, people don't get mentors unless they are serious about growing. If you truly want to do something and make a change, hurry up and show it.

After you complete your letters and before you begin the next chapter, be sure to head over to www.careerswitch.org/5review to get some more writing prompts and review what you've discovered so far.

Chapter 6
I Wrote a Letter to Slow and Urgency Wrote Me Back

"I couldn't wait for success, so I went head without it."

—Jonathan Winters

By the time you reach your late thirties and forties you have developed countless stories about what you can and can't do. These stories exist as an undercurrent in our lives that drive our decisions and keeps us safe, and when they rear their little heads we are compelled to listen to them. Some are helpful. We shouldn't be listening to most.

When it comes to your career, you may be making decisions based on faulty scripts, and if you are, it's likely that you're paying an emotional price for doing so. The most common scripts my clients come to me with are, "I'm too old," "I'd be crazy to quit my job now," "What if it doesn't work out?" or "It's too late." These scripts aren't designed to motivate us to change. They come from the part of the brain that wants to keep us safe. Keeping ourselves safe is not always a bad thing, but frequently the stories we make up to justify listening to these types of scripts paint us in a much more vulnerable place than we really are. The challenge is to figure out when to listen and when to say, "Thank you for sharing, but I have work to do."

My clients who have the easiest time flipping faulty scripts (switching them from a negative to a positive) are those who have gone through a major life event, such as the death of a friend or family member, a divorce, a firing, a crime, a profound bottoming out due to an addiction, or an accident. That's because they have experienced firsthand how quickly life can change and how precious time really is. When major life events happen, change become more urgent. In such situations, telling people close to them that they love them has to happen *now*. Moving out of a place that's been sucking the life out of them has to happen *now*. Spending the rest of their days doing work that makes them practically giddy has to happen *right now*.

For most people, however, a similar sense of urgency isn't there. It's as if there will always be more time, and when it comes to their work, unless a job has landed them in the hospital because of a complete nervous breakdown, they will tell themselves any number of stories about why they can stay, why it would be too hard to change, and why a great idea for a new job or career wouldn't work even if they tried to pursue it. Those faulty scripts cause them to be complacent.

The key to making it easier to flip your script, then, appears to be figuring out a way to create urgency about your career without having to experience a traumatic and life-altering event. Without urgency, most change efforts are doomed from the start. So how can you learn to act quickly, like your life depended on it, and be an agent of change rather than someone who waits to respond as life goes on around you?

Unfortunately, trying to create urgency when there doesn't appear to be any is difficult, which is why most people don't get moving. They think, talk, analyze, and fret until their lives are over and it finally is too late. Some people have a built-in sense of urgency. You probably know some people who conceive an idea or decide on a goal, and after that their every move is a calculated and deliberate step designed to get them to their end point quickly. They get a thought in their heads and it has to happen. That's the kind of urgency I'd like you to tap into.

When I was doing research for this book, I wanted to find out what other people said about the topic of making change and how they were overcoming the obstacle of a lack of a sense of urgency with their clients and within their own work. I sought out books and articles by psychologists and business professionals and teachers—individuals who are in the business of getting people to act and change, I was struck by how little information is out there on this topic, especially when I consider this to be the most significant barrier to career change. Certainly there are plenty of business books that talk about how to increase a sense of urgency in your managers or on your team, but how do you do it in your own life? Obvious crisis can do a lot to up the level of urgency, but barring this, major changes are usually put off until your problems becomes severe enough to generate significant losses. So we're going to start with what gets in the way of change.

I used to be a mad list maker. I would write down my goals, and then I would map out every single step in the process: every milestone, every contingency, every everything. When it came to projects like getting my thesis done, studying for my comps, or running marathons, or even writing this book, that was sort of helpful. However, those were goals I was going to achieve whether or not I had the plan for reaching them mapped out in detail. The challenge comes when you identify something you want, in this case a career change, but when you realize what it is going to take to make it happen you let complacency win.

Complacency is the enemy of change. It keeps us in a rut by preventing us from taking risks, which limits our progress.

Here's a simple graphic I have created to show you what I mean.

Figure 1 The Cycle of Complacency

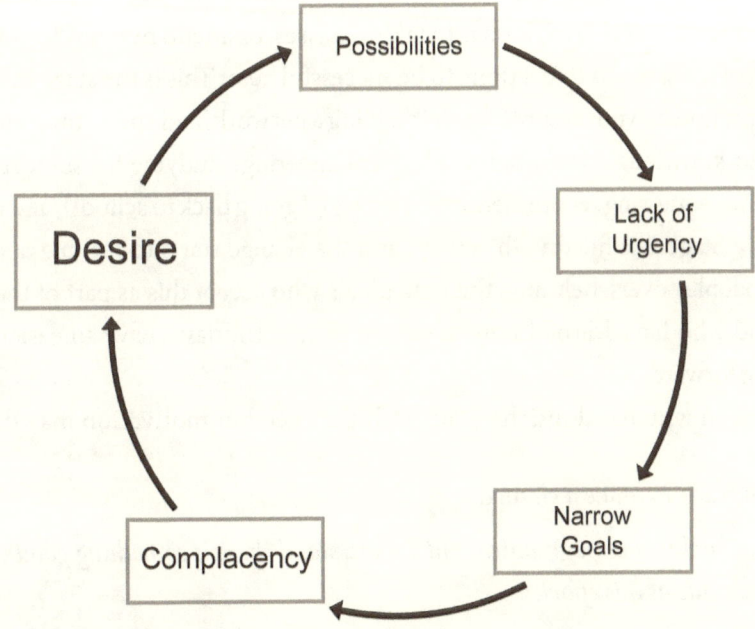

Cycle of Complacency

Possibilities

Lack of Urgency

Narrow Goals

Complacency

Desire

The Cycle of Complacency

The Cycle of Complacency has five stages.

Stage 1: Desire

In this model, you see that change begins with desire. Unless you really want to make something happen, odds are it won't. So this has to be the starting point of action. There is usually a lot of energy in this initial stage, meaning individuals are highly motivated to make a change in their careers or bring something new to life, such as a business. The urge to change careers may happen after a particularly taxing month at work, or after a year of trying to find satisfaction through volunteering, or after an especially invigorating night out with friends who were talking about the interesting work they are doing. No matter what sparks the desire, desire is the motivating force that will get you from where you are to where you want to be.

Stage 2: Explore Possibilities

In the second stage, individuals start acting on their desires and begin to research their options. They may make a list of possible careers, set up some informational interviews, look into taking classes, or attend networking events.

A lot of work needs to get done to be successful here: This is the stage in which you must update your résumé, begin building a network, and spend time increasing your knowledge or skills, including volunteering, studying for standardized tests, and requesting recommendation letters (if going back to school), and more.

While Stage 2 is filled with activity and the change starts to feel big and (for some people) overwhelming, the individuals who accept this as part of the process and who have learned how to sustain their enthusiasm have an easier time moving forward.

A person who has done the work and sustained her motivation may think:

- *I'm ready to make a change.*
- *I know this is a tough patch, but I understand there is something good on the other side of this effort.*

- *I'd better tap into my support network and get an infusion of inspiration.*

This person will take a different path (The Wave of Career Change) that leads to unlimited possibilities and growth rather than remain in the Cycle of Complacency. That process is spelled out later in the chapter.

By contrast, people who have been taken out by all of the work in Stage 2 of the Cycle of Complacency begin to notice the urgency of the situation slip away. At this point they will start focusing on the good parts of their current situations.

Stage 3: Lack of Urgency

Stage three allows the person caught in a Cycle of Complacency to compare doing all of the work she would have to do in the short term to switch jobs (which is overwhelming and difficult) to staying in her current situation (which would be comfortable and easy). The flames of her enthusiasm burn lower and smolder out.

In Stage 3 of the Cycle of Complacency, individuals will have created mental scripts like:

- *The commute is really short.*
- *My benefits are great.*
- *We couldn't make it without my paycheck and the money is nice.*
- *My boss is a cool guy.*
- *I am lucky to have such great friends at work.*

Stage 4: Narrowing of Goals

In Stage 4, people decide to narrow down their career goals to ones that can be accomplished in their current jobs. I call these Band-Aid goals, because they are designed to give people a false sense of productivity because they are doing something good and making a move toward something that would bring them more joy in their work lives. But in the end, it is only a temporary fix.

Stage 5: Complacency

In Stage 5, the prospective career changers have reached complacency. They are satisfied with their situations and have settled down to the fact that this is what work "is" and they're okay with it. They continue to focus on the benefits they get from staying where they are, and there is no reason to change, as there is no obvious crisis at hand.

Career switchers stay in Stage 5 for a short period of time, until another incident sparks another desire. The more times they go through this cycle, the shorter time they spend here. I had one client who traveled through this cycle three times before she finally popped out intact on the other side of Stage 2, rode the Wave of Career Change, and never looked back.

For some people, the original desire that is sparked in stage one is all it takes to enact a career change and they never get caught in the Cycle of Complacency. For other people, going through this process a few times is what makes it possible to have a new career.

Have you ever known a couple that used to break up a lot and then after five or more years of this decided to marry and six months later they were divorced? It happens all the time. The marriage finally created the urgency they needed to see how wrong the relationship was and they could then make the break for good.

When you fight through this complacency cycle multiple times the tension begins to build and each trip through makes you more and more ready to finally walk away from a job or a career that you don't like. When you finally leave the cycle for good it makes not only the victory of a new and satisfying career all the more sweet; it also confirms for you that it was the right thing to do.

After seeing a number of people, including myself, drift through the Cycle of Complacency many times I realized that the greatest barrier to change is a lack of urgency. I subsequently came up with all of the letters I am sharing with you in this book in addition to a solution to help you break through the barrier and, sooner rather than later, begin to do your ideal work. Once you do this, you will be riding an entirely different wave.

The Wave of Career Change: Five Steps to Raise Your Urgency Level

In Figure 2 you will see that Stage 1 and Stage 2 of the Cycle of Complacency are still there; however while the people who will get stuck in the cycle will continue on to Stage 3, "Lack of Urgency," those who are able to gain strength from the possibilities they explored in Stage 2 will pop out of the cycle and land on the Wave of Career Change and experience a successful reinvention. Once someone is on this wave there is no end point. The arrow represents unlimited possibilities. You will be able to stay on this wave by making sure you take the following five steps to raising your urgency level.

Figure 2 – Wave of Change Model

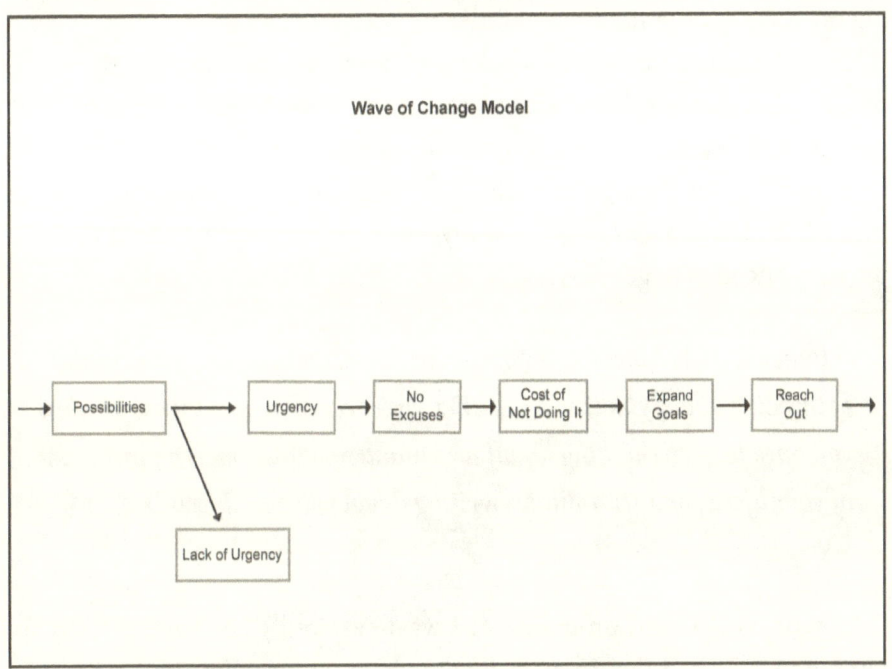

Step 1: Create a Pretend Crisis

When my daughter wants me to play Princess with her I sigh. I am not a princess and I am not the best at pretending to be aimlessly floating in the forest in my ball gown looking for Prince Charming. So, if you saw the word "pretend" and paused for a second, I don't blame you. But this is the crux of the whole thing, so bear with me.

Switching careers, when you have some decent reasons (at least in your mind) to stay in your current career, can present a challenge. It's not easy to go through a career change, so there has to be something grander motivating you than simply a desire to do better or more meaningful work. Since I don't wish a traumatic event to happen to you simply so you can change careers, I'm going to try and help you to get there another way. This is how I create a sense of urgency in my own work when one doesn't really exist. And, it is how you are going to go from Stage Two in the Cycle of Complacency to riding the wave of unlimited possibilities.

Here is a journal prompt I worked with when I was stuck in the Cycle of Complacency but desperate to get out. It's a classic journal prompt that you've probably seen or heard many times before. Even though I had also seen it before, the timing was such that it helped me to immediately shift my mindset and it changed how I saw my work and my life. It created the only urgency I needed to get moving.

> *Imagine it's Wednesday afternoon at 2 P.M. and you are in the middle of thinking about your most pressing career concern. Now, imagine that you have to keep thinking about and managing this concern for the rest of your life. Spend ten minutes writing down what that feels like.*
> *Go.*

As soon as I clicked on my timer I wrote excitedly and unabashedly for ten minutes. When the timer shrilled, I wanted more. I wanted more time to say what I felt, to get it off my chest, and to yell from the rooftops, "No, no, no—I will not cater to this struggle for the rest of my life!" It was as if by writing so feverishly that I could un-identify with my job. I could escape it, even if only for a few moments, and never be associated with it again. I had an urgent feeling. Heart beating. Palms sweating. Hands shaking. Urgent.

Here's part of that letter.

Dear Melani,

When I think about doing this work for even five more months, let alone 5 more years, I can barely breathe. I get a gigantic pit in my stomach and I feel so heavy. I feel dead.

I imagine that person five years from now and she is the walking dead. She is tired, dragging, has bags under her eyes and is barely going through the motions.

She is dumb. She got dumb because she thought it would be safer to keep doing inane work. She got dumb because she thought getting paid great to do shitty work was a better deal than being paid less for doing awesome work. That is really frickin dumb!

She has sold her soul for the money and she's weak. She's out of integrity, out of control and out of voice.

I can't let that be me. I can't teach that lesson to my daughter. I can't. I won't.

How is it possible that I can so clearly see the way through for my clients but I haven't seen it for me? That's not true. I can see it; I just haven't been able to do it.

That's worse maybe. Far worse.

I want to do something I care about. I can't stand giving lip service to it anymore.

I declare that I will not be doing this work five months from now. This pit will be gone, the work will be a memory and this conversation will be over. I will feel relieved.

Get out now!

From the You that Knows What You Need to Do Right Now

Once I came down from the emotional high and closed my battered and frayed journal, I realized that my reaction was my inner self desperately calling out for some attention. This was not the response of a girl who just didn't like her job. This was the response of a girl who knew, in the deep recesses of her mind, that there was something she wanted to do and was not doing. It was about feeling out of integrity, out of control, and out of time.

The key part about this anecdote is that I had already been through the Cycle of Complacency more times than I'd care to admit. I also had really good reasons to stay at my job: Zero commute (I worked from home), great money, no travel, work I had a knack for doing very well, flexible hours, and lots of freedom to spend time with my daughter and other family members. Those are perks that most people would love to include as part of their job description, and they are the reasons I had continued on the same career trajectory far longer than I ever should have. However, imagining myself rolling around in this unhappiness, with it ever present in my mind even six months from then, let alone for the rest of my life, was too much to bear. I could see myself years down the road and it was not a pretty picture. I decided that all of the uncertainty, difficulties, and challenges that go along with a career change were nothing compared to how badly I would feel if I was still fretting about it a year later.

That was how I created urgency for my own career change. That one simple journal prompt moved me forward as quickly as real life tragedies had moved me in the past. In fact, here's what I did as soon as I finished responding to that prompt.

1. I took a look at all of my expenses and figured out exactly what I needed to make to stay in the black and not starve.
2. I figured out how much I needed to save so that I could quit by a certain date.
3. I immediately took steps to revive my old copywriting business so I could increase my income while I was trying to save.
4. I began marketing to get copy clients and planned my next steps.
5. I reached out to mentors, colleagues, and friends to get support. I told people about my ideas. I told them about my deadlines. I told my best friend to call me on my shit when I make excuses—she's really good at that.

Basically I made a declaration to those closest to me, to myself, and to the Universe about what I wanted and the kind of support I thought I needed to make it happen, preferably in the now timeframe. There was no getting off the wave at that point.

When you consider the time you have in your life and you move your lens from right in front of you to further into the future, urgency can be created spontaneously simply from facing the prospect of future disappointment, regret, pain, and suffering.

Step 2: Eliminate Justification and Excuses

Excuses are simply our attempt to reduce our personal responsibility for actions we take. Justifications are what we use to prove our excuses are sound. It's a nasty pairing that gets us into a lot of trouble. When it comes to not going after the career we want, our excuses, such as, *I barely have enough time to get my job done and do what I need to do at home. I'll never have time to figure out a career change,* serve as barriers to getting what we want. In this example, we are saying that the reason we can't change careers is because we don't have time. The real reason is more along the lines of "It's going to take too much work" or "I don't know how to do it" or "I don't know where to start."

A list of excuses is like a chain, and if you want to stop letting excuses be your barrier to change, then you have to learn how to break the chain. Here's how.

First, write down what you want to happen. For example: "I want to go back to school and earn a Ph.D."

Then fill in the blanks in these sentences:

- I can't go back to school because of X.

- I can't do X because of Y.

- I can't do Y because of Z.

Finally, examine your chain. I guarantee there's a weak link in there somewhere. Take out the link and see what happens to your excuses. Having a tool to help get you out of moving forward will come in handy when you simply don't have time to get taken out. This tool has kept me on the wave on more than one occasion.

Step 3: Calculate the Cost of Not Accomplishing the Goal

This one is pretty simple, yet it's a step that's frequently missed. When career change gets difficult, we concentrate on all of the reasons we don't really need to change and stay focused on those reasons because it's easier than reminding ourselves of why we want to change. If however, you focus on the cost of not changing your career now, or of not at least taking a step in the direction of change, you will have the information you need to make a better decision.

Think about what your current career is costing you. Maybe you are so unhappy with your job that you get sick a lot, you're cranky, you're irritable, you hate the work you're doing, you have terrible insomnia, you feel trapped, and your talents are being wasted. Maybe you work a hundred hours a week, your commute is taxing, or your role does not allow for any creativity or advancement. Imagine how you feel right now in this moment, and calculate what five more years of this activity would do to you. Or even one more year. How will continuing to work in that role and in that environment impact your health, your relationships, your sense of self and accomplishment?

Now, imagine yourself in your new and more fulfilling career. It's three years from now and you are doing the work you've dreamed of doing? What has changed?

Is the cost you will incur in the short term through doing the work it takes to change your career path worth it, considering all of the negative consequences you will have to endure if you stay in your current job? I suspect your answer is a resounding yes—and that affirmation should give you enough urgency and inspiration to keep you going.

Step 4: Expand Your Goals to Those that Cannot Be Met Without Significant Change

One of the best pieces of advice I've ever heard on the subject of goals was to make them big enough that I would have to change my life in some way in order to achieve them, but not so big that they were out of reach. When we have to change who we are and what we are doing to accomplish something, then we are forced to get out of our comfort zones. We are forced to take a look at the obstacles that get in our way, to see how we sabotage ourselves, and to discover the tricks we come up with to stay in the game. When we set goals for ourselves that are a stretch and require us to change, we also create built-in urgency. We can't go slowly and plod along like we have been because these types of goals demand more of us.

There's a learning curve involved in expanding your goals. As soon as you start participating in the process of moving out of your comfort zone, you change who you are. When you change who you are, the *status quo* is no longer an option. You create a new normal for the kind of person you are and the kind of person you want to be.

When I was a marketing consultant, I had a client whose goal was to make a million dollars in her business. I would press her about it, asking her why over and over again, and she would only say that this was the number that would make her feel satisfied and accomplished. The problem was that no matter how much planning and strategizing she did, and no matter how many items she put on her to-do list to get there, she never even took a step. It was too gigantic and nebulous a goal. She was making far less than six figures, and the million-dollar goal was merely a number that sounded good in her head.

Eventually this client decided to adjust her goal. Her new goal was still a stretch for her, but it was definitely doable. At first it was a difficult switch to make because it was more realistic. That meant that if she failed to accomplish her goal she could no longer blame the fact that it was too big. It also meant that she was going to have to make some deliberate changes in how she spent her time if she had any chance of reaching her goal. Even so, she told me that the minute she adjusted her goal her heart started beating and she could not get to work fast enough. It was big enough to get her excited and motivated, and not so big that she would give up. Retrospectively she says, "The plan to get there didn't change, but the urgency did."

Step 5: Enlist the Support of Others

As I indicated in Chapter 3, none of us can do this alone. We need to surround ourselves with a great network of support. When it comes to creating urgency, the principle is no different. Our friends and family can be the voice of reason when we start to slip off the path of progress and head back to our comfortable jobs. They remind us of what we said to them that night on the phone when we told them through tears, "This time really is going to be different." They send us back to our research when we want to give up and watch TV. And when we come home crabby and irritable from a typical day at work, they mirror our pain back to us and remind us that it's not only about us anymore, it's about everyone in our lives.

The key to getting appropriate support is telling people what you need. Give them a list of your deadlines—telling them what you are going to do and when—and ask them to hold you accountable. Show your kids what you are doing and why you are doing it, and let them play Principal for a while. When I tell my six-year old daughter I have to finish an article, later, when I am reading or watching TV, she will ask me, "Mommy, did you finish your article?" If I say no, she'll say, "But you said you were going to finish it before you did anything else." Then, because I'm acting like a loser for not doing what I said I was going to do, I go back to my desk. (Yes. That entire conversation actually happened, and yes, my daughter was thrilled that she was able to call me out.)

Supportive friends and family, including concerned little ones, can do a lot to create urgency for us when we start to nose dive off the wave and fall back into the Cycle of Complacency. They are the ones who believe in us when we start to doubt ourselves, and they are the ones who will be our loudest cheerleaders at the end. They will also be the ones, aside from ourselves, who benefit most when we begin doing the work we love.

WRITE THAT SH*T DOWN

Now it's time for you to practice creating urgency on your path to career clarity.

Priming the Pump

Imagine it's Wednesday afternoon at 2 P.M. and you are at work, and you're in the middle of a project you've been working on for a few weeks. Now, imagine that you have to keep doing this work for the rest of your life.

Spend ten minutes writing down what that feels like.

If you are not currently working, but wish you were, imagine you are doing whatever it is you are doing now for the next five or ten years. What would that be like?

Go.

Write a Letter to Urgency

Now that you have spent time writing down what it would be like to do the work you are currently doing, it's time to write a letter to Urgency. Tell it why your career change has to happen now. Tell it what you need so that you can pursue it right now. Identify any barriers you need to break down, any stale excuses that keep you from moving quickly, and anything your inner critic is saying that needs to be silenced.

Don't be afraid to ask for what you need and to name what you will do if you get it. Make promises. Imagine this is the only chance you have.

Play with It

Now, you have to do something to sustain your enthusiasm and maintain that level of urgency. The best way to do that is to reach out for support. Make yourself accountable by enlisting the help of other people.

A few months ago my friends took me out to celebrate my birthday. While I was on my way to the restaurant I had this idea that we should go around the table and each say something we needed support on, whether we needed people to be collectively thinking about us while we were trying to accomplish it or we were looking for some specific accountability during the process. This little idea turned into one of the most entertaining nights I've ever had. One of my friends had the great idea to "shazam" each person after they announced their single, hairiest, scariest goal. Pretty soon our shazams could be heard throughout the restaurant. I am not a loud person so drawing attention to myself in this way is not how I'd normally choose to spend my time; however, while I was in the moment I had a sense this was going to be a night we wouldn't forget for a long time. The next day one of my friends emailed the list to all of us so we could keep these eight goals in our minds. That evening's shazam combined with a lot of action and effort allowed us to achieve many of the goals we shared that night. My goal was to write this book. They helped me make this happen. With the support of others, you can make your most magnificent goals happen, too.

So, if you're comfortable doing so, share your letter to Urgency with people you trust. Or even parts of the letter. Most people are happy to serve as accountability partners, and by letting them see your "why," the source of your passion and commitment to the process, they will be excited to take the ride with you.

Be specific about what you need (you would like them to call you once a week, you would prefer weekly email nudges) and what you plan to do (you will deliver a chapter a week of your book, or you will research five companies you want to work for and write up a summary of each one). If you do not tell them what you want and what you are going to do, the relationship can quickly fail to serve you and can burden them.

After you complete your letters and before you begin the next chapter, be sure to head over to www.careerswitch.org/6review to get some more writing prompts and review what you've discovered so far.

· ·

Chapter 7
I Wrote a Letter to Desire and Passion Wrote Me Back

"Don't be the person who is out there looking for a job. Be the person who is out there doing something interesting."

—Jeanne Schad

Getting good first is how passion develops. I recently attended an event put on by the *Unreasonable Institute* in Boulder, Colorado, where six of their "Unreasonable Fellows" gave five-minute presentations about the work they were doing to solve the world's biggest problems. One presenter, a woman who has spent the past twelve years studying poop, was a stand out. Ashley Murray's work involves changing the way the world does sanitation. She says, "By using human waste as the primary feedstock for other products, we harness its resource value, successfully restructuring the financial incentives that have failed human waste collection, treatment, and disposal in the developing world."[1]

During the presentation, Ashley talked about her work in Ghana and Kenya, and her plans to scale her solution to reach countries all over the world. Her excitement was so contagious that everyone in the room felt it. As soon as it was over, I reached out to her to see if she would talk to me about her work. Her passion was obvious, yet I was confident that being immersed in fecal matter all day was not the kind of work anyone would sit home dreaming about as a career—her original motivations had to be something as yet unknown to me—so I wanted to find out more about her story.

It turns out that I guessed right: Fecal matter was not the work on which Ashley had set her sights. Her career exploration began when she was nineteen years old and decided to take a year off from college to figure out what she wanted to do before she became stuck in a rut in the wrong career. She read *The Back Door Guide to Short-term Job Adventures,* a book by Michael Landes (Ten Speed Press, 2000), which she says changed her life. It helped her so much that she recommends it to all of the young people she meets. It led her to Sarasota, Florida, to work in the field of marine biology, where she learned quickly that this was not the career for her.

Ashley then applied to *Alliances Abroad,* an organization that creates cultural exchange experiences and places young people in unpaid internships and volunteer positions, and paid positions and teaching roles all over the world. She was placed in Ghana. While she was teaching high school biology and chemistry, living in that country opened her eyes to what was really happening regarding water and waste—and having deeply cared about the environment her whole life, this was a problem she could really get behind solving.

Ashley ended up going back to school and studying abroad in China during her junior year. After she graduated, she worked for another year in China studying waste water systems, and then went back to school and earned a master's degree in civil and environmental engineering in 2005. She continued her training after that program to receive a doctorate from the Energy and Resources Group at the University of California, Berkeley in 2009. While working on her doctoral dissertation, she spent most of her time in China, again researching waste water systems and how they could be designed for reuse. While she loved the work she did, she realized that when it came to reusing waste, China was going to be a lost cause. The Chinese were doing everything they could just to manage the waste they had, and she felt that she was never going to be able to change their direction toward *reusing* the waste.

As a result of this insight, she realized that if she was ever going to be able to sell anyone on her ideas of reusing waste, she was going to have to make a financial case for it. She has made her case to governments, banks, and nonprofit organizations so well over the years that today her company, *Waste Enterprisers,* is on the verge of massive growth. The company is replacing the outmoded concept of disposal-oriented treatment with a technology and a business model for producing biodiesel fuel from fecal sludge. The systems Ashley and her colleagues have invented for converting fecal sludge into reusable energy have gone through rigorous testing. Their company has the backing of some the chief players out there, organizations such as the *International Finance Corporation* and the *Bill and Melinda Gates Foundation,* and they set up their full production in Ghana during summer 2012, with a goal to scale it and ramp up capacity over the next several years in Sub-Saharan Africa.

Fecal sludge is this woman's life. Ashley lights up when she talks about it, and her energy is palpable. We met for coffee on a beautiful summer morning and she told me all about her work. I never imagined that fecal sludge could bring me to the edge of my seat, but it did. When I asked her how she keeps going when she considers what a giant problem this is, she said, "I'm chronically optimistic." When pressed, she said that the idea of stopping or backing off doesn't ever occur to her. She said that "Everyone has fecal sludge and everyone needs fuel. This is a problem I can solve, and I'm so convinced it will work that stopping is not an option."

I was struck by how sure she was and how much her certainty and belief were driving her. Talking to her made it even more clear to me that in order for you to do your ideal work, the kind of work that adds meaning to your life, is interesting to you, and requires you to use the best of who you are, you have to first believe in the impact you are going to make and believe that *you* can make it. Twelve years ago Ashley had a strong desire to explore the world, so strong that she acted on it by taking a year off of school. She tested out options and searched for the thing she couldn't wait to get out of bed to do. She discovered a problem that lit a fire under her and she felt the urgency of it every day. No matter how enormous the problem appeared to be, she took steps to maintain her enthusiasm, and stayed involved and today she is solving a global problem, and doing it quite handily at that. Ashley did not discover her passion by reading a book or taking a test, she discovered it by acting on a desire and by putting herself in situations where opportunities would present themselves to her. Now passion for her work oozes out of her in every breath.

Many people who talk about finding their passion or figuring out what they are here to do (as if there was, in fact, one thing) believe this thing is something that can be thought into being. They will make lists and wait around and continue doing work they hate, hoping that the passion piece of their job puzzle will magically show up one day.

That's not how it works.

Passion can't be found from a list on a page. Or by setting an intention and taking zero actions to generate results. It is found by getting good at something, like Ashley did. The desire comes first, then actions on behalf of that desire. Hopefully passion, the experience we have when we love doing a particular activity or engaging with ideas, comes next. As the famous educational reformer John Dewey wrote, "You need to catch interest before you can hold on to it."[2]

My husband, Chris, and I regularly have conversations comparing the merits of doing whatever you can that pays the bills with doing what you love. Chris is a super-practical guy, who sees his job and his career as a means to an end. His job pays the bills, allows him to have plenty of time with his family, and allows him to live in one of the best spots in the country. It's hard to argue with that. Of course, I do it anyway.

I am one of those people for whom working any old job sounds like a thousand shades of awful. I'll do it if I have to, but I sure don't like the idea. When Chris asks me what I want from my work, I rattle off a litany of requirements: It should be useful, interesting, meaningful, challenging, and fun, and impact a lot of people. It should revolve around a craft and topic I can master, something I am proud to talk about, and, oh yes, I also want to make money doing it. (It's no wonder it took me so long to pop out on the other side of stage two and leave the Cycle of Complacency.)

Chris looks at me like I'm nuts when we have these conversations. But there's a part of him that also knows finding work that meets those requirements is not such a bad idea. As long as the money piece is ranked further at the top!

Recently when we had one of these conversations, we talked about all of the career advice we've heard from our parents and in graduation speeches and on the news, and we both came to the same conclusion: Nobody agrees on how you should choose your work.

When I was contemplating doctoral programs there was a popular saying among my professors. They would say, "For every dissertation on the shelves there's another one that refutes it." I'm not sure if that was meant to chill me out and make me see that, as significant a project as it was for me, my dissertation was not going to be the definitive work on the subject, or of my life, but it was a tad discouraging to hear. All of that work, only to be placed on the bookshelf next to another paper that suggests the opposite? Yet, every time I read books on career, I am reminded of what my professors said and I am struck by how disparate the advice in the career change field is when it comes to making a change.

- Follow your passion first
- Following your passion is nonsense
- Hold out for meaningful work
- Get a job that pays, as any job will be equally good for you
- Make a Venn diagram
- Don't make a Venn diagram
- Work for free
- Don't ever work for free
- It's all about doing the inner work first
- Doing inner work and analysis will get you nowhere
- Concentrate on what motivates you intrinsically
- Extrinsic motivation is critical to finding a job you'll love
- Holding out for work you love is selfish
- Not holding out for work you love will cause you to be depressed, anxious, and a miserable person to be around

- A personality test holds all of the answers
- Personality tests are bunk when it comes to looking for the right career

What is a career seeker or a career changer supposed to do with all of this conflicting advice? Who do you believe? Where do you start?

For myself, I decided to start by talking to as many people as I could who had actually navigated a successful career change and found a passion they never knew they had.

Here are a few of the insights I gained from my research.

- Finding your passion and finding your dream job are entirely different things. Unless you can hit the sweet spot between what you love to do and what you can get paid to do, that passion may be better off as your side gig.

- When you have a strong desire to make something happen, like a career change (and you don't have unlimited support and finances to make it happen for you), you will compromise sleep, BBQs, vacations, weekends off, reality TV, and luxuries to make it happen.

- Career change is 75 percent about what's out there already and 25 percent about what you can create out of nothing. Don't be afraid of the 25%.

- Most of the time you won't know if you truly love doing something unless you've done it for a while. Meaning that we develop a passion for something only after we get good at it. Passion does not come from just thinking about what sounds cool or interesting or exciting. A *desire* is sparked, which gets us moving to do the work, but the passion for that work develops over time.

- As long as the work you are doing does not go *against* your values (even though it may not match your top values), simply doing work itself, having a job, and making a contribution will add value to your life. Having some work to do will likely give you the breathing room you need to go after the work you *care* about.

- We are not good predictors of what motivates us or what we'll enjoy doing. Testing is critical.

- Loving what you do and doing what you love are not the same things. They are two different mindsets.

If all of this is true, what does one do to find the right fit? Where does clarity come from, aside from writing letters of course? From *experimentation*. Exploring possibilities is stage two in the Cycle of Complacency.

Many people have an aversion to experiments because they don't like the uncertainty of their outcomes or the risk that accompanies them. Most of the experiments that we conduct in the world of work leave the potential for surprise, and as much as we think we like them, we kind of don't. Surprises, uncertainty, and instability—they make most of us nervous, so when something as significant as our career choice is on the line, then the aversion becomes even greater.

But this is where the fun happens: Surprise makes life interesting. If you search for a life that has no tension, one that is scripted and obvious and safe, then very little in it will be satisfying. Experiments can remind you that you are in the game and you get to call the shots.

When we consider how averse so many people are to uncertainty, it is no wonder that the principal mistake people make when they are contemplating a career change is hesitating to step forward. They want to be sure they are doing the right thing, they want to do all the research, and they want to make sure their direction is clear and logical. They don't want to get lost. The problem is that they'll never know if they are doing the right thing if they don't simply start doing it. Julien Smith writes in *The Flinch*, "Getting lost is not fatal. Almost every time, it will make your world bigger."[3] I agree. You must be willing to get lost in order to find your way.

When I was going through a career change, I knocked out four possibilities by doing experiments. As my husband would attest, experimenting is my preferred method of inquiry because I'm not a fan of sitting back and wasting time. When I get a nudge or something sparks my interest, I usually take the next step right away. Thus, my experiments have included volunteering, working on the side, interning, and taking classes. I did all of these experiments without compromising the paying job I had at the time, which was a critical piece of my transition process.

Chucking stability to experiment can be a dangerous game because when you are under the gun financially or there's pressure to make something new work out for you, you won't think as clearly and you're more likely to jump to commitment too soon.

Did all of the experimenting while I was still working my "day job" cost me some time and some money? Absolutely. However, it also saved me even more time and the pain of going down wrong pathways of possibility.

One of the jobs that I thought about doing was nursing. I loved the idea of doing a job that was necessary and useful and where I would spend the entire day helping people. I wanted to work in a chaotic and urgent atmosphere where there was no time to rest. I loved the idea of working three or four nights a week and having days to myself (since I rarely sleep anyway). Also, maybe more than anything, I wanted to have a skill and do something with my hands. I wanted to do something tangible that had immediate outcomes and was easy to explain. So I decided one day to get my feet wet. I started taking nursing classes and began volunteering in the local ER.

Six weeks into my experiment I realized that nursing was absolutely the wrong career path for me. Here's something I wrote after I spent a few weeks volunteering in the ER.

Dear Nursing,

I think you are the absolute wrong fit for me. And by "wrong fit" I mean I would not last ten minutes in this field.

Each day that I am in the ER instead of being drawn to help the patients that come to the hospital, I'm drawn to help the families of the patients. Instead of loving my classes and the fact that all of the problems I'm trying to solve have definitive answers, I miss my psychology classes, where we used to discuss and debate possible answers for hours. Instead of loving the time I am there all I want to do is get home and write. Sometimes I don't even wait until I get home. I just sit in my car and write before I even turn the car on.

However, when I think about walking away I get nervous to give something up that is so clearly defined for something that's so vague, like writing.

On the other hand, when I think about all of the reasons I wanted to get into nursing (schedule, environment, work product) I realize I could experience all of that by working at a magazine, not that I could get hired these days BUT the reality of it is that nursing is not the thing. The other things are the thing. Shocker.

How can I bring some of that into my writing life?

- Join a writer's group. (Be part of something.)
- Take on more copywriting clients and get a column with a strict due date. (Get more deadlines and be busier.)
- Pitch and get published in a print magazine I'd want to buy.
- Write a book about career. (Produce something I can hold in my hands.)
- Focus some of my writing on topics related to the other parts of my career such as communication and conflict resolution so that I can bring the two together more.

I can do all of those things. But I haven't. I think it's because if I don't do everything I want to do with my writing then I'll get to keep the dream alive. I can always keep the fantasy in my head, "If I really gave it everything I've got then I could be a successful writer." That's a nice fantasy to have. And, if I decide to stop creating all of these ridiculous distractions for myself and actually give my writing 100 percent and I don't succeed, then I have to face a different reality. And that one doesn't sound fun at all.

But holding back is its own version of hell, too.

What would get to change for me if I didn't think that trying and failing was the worst thing on the planet? Chances are I would still fail but I'd probably succeed a lot too. I'm going to focus on that part for a while.

Tomorrow, I write.

Melani

Trying out different options when you are contemplating a career change is the single best way to determine whether or not something is a fit. With each experiment you do, you become clearer on your priorities, you answer questions you didn't even know you had, and the momentum you create from that experiment will lead to even more action, as you make your way toward the career path that is new and exciting and interesting to you. In Chapter 2, we talked about "if only." Experiments help you consider "what if?"

Something critical to remember when you are contemplating a career change is that it's not purely an intellectual decision, it's an emotional one, too. During each experiment you try you will be inclined to make a move based on your emotions. When you have been stuck in a career that is a mismatch for you and you're wasted and fed up with your current situation, or when you've been out of work for a long time, the moment you enter into new territory it feels fresh and exciting. It's easy to get taken in then, and not see the whole picture. You therefore have to be sure that you bring the emotional responses together with the objective and intellectual side of you to make the best decision. If you put reason behind your emotions you will create a better space for you to make a decision.

So, take your time, consider all the possibilities available to you, and give yourself permission to have fun playing in the sandbox for a while. Your ability to sustain your enthusiasm throughout the experimentation process will determine whether or not you move forward with a greater sense of urgency, or you decide it's too much work and any sense of urgency you had dwindles out. When this happens you get caught in the cycle again until you are hit by another desire.

When Should You Cut Your Losses?

During a cognitive psychology class I once took, we addressed this question: *When someone has a high desire to do something, but an apparently low aptitude for it, at what point, if any, do you steer them in another direction?* We were talking about this as teachers would—teaching being a role in which we might desire to steer a student in another direction.

Right now, we're talking about you and how you can solve your career dilemmas. Your concern is: How do you know when to cut your losses, either because a job experiment is not going as you had hoped or because you show no aptitude for the work? What do you do if the idea of a profession sounded good and in practice it turns out to be a really bad fit? How do you know when you should stick with an experiment and persevere a while longer?

In *The Dip* (Portfolio, 2007), marketing expert Seth Godin says, "Extraordinary benefits accrue to the tiny majority of people who are able to push just a tiny bit longer than most. Extraordinary benefits also accrue to the tiny majority with the guts to quit early and refocus their efforts on something new. In both cases, it's about being the best in the world. About getting through the hard stuff and coming out on the other side."[4] Godin says that whenever we start something new we get hung up on the fun of it. We keep going because of the great feedback we get and because all the learning we do makes us feel good. This learning keeps us engaged . . . until we reach the dip, the long trudge that exists between novice and master.[5] The dip is the point between beginner's luck and real accomplishment, and it's designed to keep the majority of people out.

On the other side of the story, according to Godin, is the cul de sac. This is when you realize that no amount of work is going to change the situation. You can't get in a groove, you're constantly failing at a key piece of the puzzle, and you extract virtually no joy from the endeavor. It's a dead end.

I can't tell you how long it takes to reach this point in a given career experiment, but you'll know it when you get there. The decision to give up on a particular career avenue is not about backing out because it's hard and challenging or because it's taking up a lot of time as well as effort. This is not about being able to see a bright future and yet quitting now because the pain in the moment is too much to bear. This is about a dead end that you feel in your bones. You're traveling a road that you know is leading you to a place where you will never be able to be extraordinary.

I didn't quit my path to nursing because it was too difficult; I quit it because it was the absolute wrong fit for me in about ten different ways. I knew that if I quit it right then I would have the time and attention I needed to focus on something that was a better fit. There is nothing wrong with experiments not working, and wouldn't you much rather find out that the career is not a good fit for you through an experiment than after you had left a paying job or steady gig behind to pursue it?

If there is something you've wanted to quit, but haven't, what's holding you back? Why are you afraid of quitting? Write down the first thing that comes to mind, and each time you think you have the answer ask "why?" again. Keep going until you drill down to the truth.

Try Outs

The following are some quick examples of people who participated in experiments to see what would stick.

The Intern

Stacey was a teacher who had dreams of spending her days working with adults. She was getting burned out by all of the politics at school and all of the time and energy she had to spend preparing for standardized tests. Plus she had two little kids of her own and she felt like she was so exhausted from working with other kids all day that by the time her kids had her attention she didn't have enough of herself to give. Her guilt was wearing her out. She thought if she could somehow find a teaching job with adults that she could still do what she was best at, she would be able to focus more on real world content and then still have energy for her own kids at the end of the day.

Through a fellow teacher and friend she was put in touch with a woman who headed a training department for a mid-sized company. They did not have many full-time trainers so they were always looking for more hands on deck. Stacey sent the head of the department a proposal for a two-month internship that she could do during her summer vacation and they accepted. (An essential lesson to be gained from this is that there was no intern position advertised. Stacey created the proposal and told them why she could help them and they accepted.)

During the summer Stacey fell in love with the work. Her days, while mostly filled with preparing for trainings and even delivering some, were also filled with other activities she loved such as researching and writing, two activities she didn't have much time to do while she was teaching in the classroom. She had already committed to another year at her school and she didn't want to break her contract but she left her internship with some great contacts and made a promise to herself that she would spend the next year looking for a job in a training department. She also promised herself that even if a job offer did not come by the time contracts were sent out again in the spring, she would not sign the contract. She had to make a statement that she wanted something different.

She wasn't able to secure a job offer before she received her contract for the next school year, but she kept her promise and didn't sign. She ended up in another company the following summer helping to organize their training materials, and by the end of the summer they offered her a full-time position. She loves her new job and so does her family. She says that had she not taken the initiative and written that proposal she would probably still be in her old job, wrecked and exhausted.

Lesson: The world is not waiting to put you in your dream job. You have to make it happen.

The Volunteer

My dear friend Amy was a photographer who entered the field for the love of the art form. This was at a time when digital didn't exist and only the best photographers were able to make a good living doing it. She attended Parsons School of Design in New York City and soon was a sought-after photographer doing both commercial and portrait photography. She loved the work and loved the art form, and coming from a family where everyone worked as an artist in some form or fashion, she felt right at home in her work.

Then digital came along and the photography world started to change. The work began to change, the competition became stiffer now that everyone on the block had access to great cameras and great tools that could make them a better photographer than they probably were, and Amy began to lose her enthusiasm for her work.

When her first child was born she started considering other options she might explore while she continued to maintain her freelance photography business. Eventually her second child was born and her thoughts about what she was going to do next became more urgent. At the recommendation of her mother and her aunt she decided to look into sonography. Amy had always been what she called "med curious" and as an EMT and volunteer fire-fighter the idea of going into medicine of some type always interested her. With sonography she would be able to bring together her loves of medicine and of imaging in a way she had never imagined. She also loved the idea of working in a busy hospital where having multiple conversations with the same people on a regular basis was the norm. She had been starting to feel iso-lated in her freelance business because even though she would communicate with her subjects, all of the work she did outside of the shoot to touch up the pictures and market herself was a solitary endeavor. Isolation wasn't a condi-tion she thrived in.

Amy began looking into programs and volunteering at hospitals to see what the work would be like. She fell in love with it immediately. I remember her calling me one day after she had spent ten hours studying for a physics test and telling me, "I could not love physics any more than I do." Hearing the sound of her voice so filled with excitement was wonderful. Then finally after volunteering and finishing all of her pre-requisites she was admitted to her first choice school. We spoke two weeks before she would begin classes.

Amy said that the most noteworthy shift for her was being able to let go of her creative identity. There was always something she loved about being seen as a creative person and whenever she told people she was a photographer their ears perked up. It was difficult to let that go, but once she realized how fulfilling it was to do this work, she was ready to go for-ward full steam ahead. She said, "I can't believe it took me so long to put this together but I'm pretty sure that I was meant to do this work. I'm so grateful that I had someone looking out for me or I may never have seen what was right in front of me all along."

Lesson: Tell people who love you what you're up to and what's on your mind as it relates to your career goals. Be open to their ideas and be willing to experiment even when you don't know if it will work out. Volunteering is one of the best paths you can take to investigate a new career because even if it doesn't work out, you've still given of yourself and for that you will get much in return.

The Risk Taker

Jason was thirty-eight-years old when he decided to quit his corporate job and become a health coach and trainer. He was burned out on his career and had an idea for what he wanted to do, but was too scared to make it happen. Having worked in corporate America since he finished graduate school four-teen years earlier he had become accustomed to a certain lifestyle and he liked being seen as smart and successful. He kept his ideas about wanting to be a health coach and trainer to himself for a long time because he was afraid of what people would think. He felt he had already "messed up his marriage" because he hadn't been able to balance a demanding job with anything else in his life.

When his wife left him he went through a terrible bout of depression. What finally turned his life around was reconnecting to his love of health and fit-ness, something that he had put on the back burner for nearly a decade. Soon he was running marathons and ultra-marathons again, going to the gym, and meeting new people who were into the same activities he was. As he did, his life was getting better.

The only problem was that while Jason was feeling vibrant and alive in one part of his life, his work was draining him. He had no passion left and he didn't understand how he could now loathe something he at one time had loved so much that he couldn't wait to get to work.

He had a conversation with one of his training partners one day and after Jason had told him his ideas his friend said, "You would be a really great coach and trainer. Look at what you've accomplished. You should give it a try." Jason felt encouraged by his friend but the thought of dipping his toe in while he was still at his job felt too heavy and overwhelming. Plus, he didn't think it would be congruent if he was preaching one thing to his clients and he wasn't living it himself. He made the bold decision to quit his job with no safety net. He had no idea if he would be able to pull off his new business idea or even if anyone would want what he had to sell. All he had was a deep desire to do it.

Fortunately it turned out to be enough. Well, that combined with a lot of hustling. As he had hoped Jason became a health coach and trainer who works with male executives all over the world, helping them do exactly what he did: find the time to eat well and take care of their bodies no matter how crazy and stressful their day. While he does get paid well, it is nowhere near what he made in his old job. Even so, he is one hundred times happier. These days he looks back on the person he was five years ago and he says he can't blame his wife for leaving him. He would have left him, too.

Lesson: Sometimes the only way to shake an old identity is to leave it behind completely. This is not always possible or financially feasible if you have bills to pay and mouths to feed and no reserve; however, if it is, it can be the best way to create a sense of urgency and move quickly into exactly the work you want to do.

From Curiosity to Passion

One thing that all the aforementioned people doing tryouts had in common is that they were curious enough about a possible path to do something about it. Curiosity motivates us and holds our attention. It's our growth point. When you approach your experiments with the lens of curiosity, your ability to remain engaged will open you up to a whole new set of possibilities you likely never would have considered before you began.

As you read in the previous examples of Stacey, Amy, and Jason, we learn who we are by practicing, not by thinking about who we are—not in theory. The bulk of the work we have to do in a career reinvention is *not* up front. If you are actually doing what I suggest in this book then you are probably reading and writing 25 percent of the time and *doing* 75 percent of the time, which is exactly how it should be. You are not going to find your dream job or ideal career, or even your passion, doing it any other way.

The way we learn about ourselves is by doing and then observing how we react to what crosses our path. The moment you say yes to acting on the desire you have for a certain career path you invite the possibility for passion to come in. That is one of the best gifts you can ever give yourself. Passion needs room to flow. By experimenting and committing to something "as if" it were your new career you give passion a place to land.

It's possible that after you start the experiment you'll feel stuck and scared and have thoughts of "OMG! What did I get myself into?" That's okay. You haven't really committed, you've only tricked yourself into thinking you have. That's why it's not a good idea to quit your current paying job and hope everything works out okay. On the other hand, you may be so enthralled by what you're doing that you'll wonder, like Amy did, what took you so long to take a step. This is all good information.

Experiments help us get clear. We have wild and vivid imaginations, and whether we are considering relationships, vacations, careers, or anything else, we believe we are masters at predicting how something is going to be. We are rarely correct, however. We incorrectly predict the reality of many situations and we also incorrectly predict how we will feel about them. That's why experiments are such a critical piece of the career change process.

I say throw predictions out the door when it comes to your career. They won't get you where you want to go, which is to being excited, interested, and committed to your new path.

Listen to Your Body

"Respect the fact that it is possible to know without knowing we know and accept that—sometimes—we're better off that way."

—Malcolm Gladwell

Before I send you off to do your experiments I want to stress the importance of listening to your body when it comes to your work and career reinvention.

As I said in Chapter 1, when I was doing work I hated my body was giving me warning signals left and right. I was getting sick a lot. As soon as I would get over one bug another would come along. I contracted laryngitis more times than I can count (if that is not a warning sign that I was slowly giving up my "voice" I don't know what is). I could not sleep, going weeks and weeks without being able to sleep through the night, and my stomach always felt like it was in knots. The really crazy thing about it is that on paper I've always been remarkable healthy. I wasn't overweight, I didn't eat unhealthy foods, and I worked out rigorously nearly every day. However, all of the healthy habits I'd been practicing since I was a little kid were no match for the stress and unhappiness that made up so much of my life at that time. Since I shut down my marketing consulting business, I have not been sick once, which makes it even easier to do the work I love.

When it's time to start considering the different types of experiments you might try, as I am going to have you do in the next Priming the Pump exercise, I want you to play close attention to how your body responds to the ideas that come to mind. Here's a fact that I resisted for a long time: Our bodies are much less complicated than our brains. Our brains like to analyze every last piece of information they get. The brain wants to sort, categorize, compare, and make sense of everything. However, our bodies are designed to focus on the essential, in-the-moment information. The body doesn't care about percentages and cost benefit charts and all of that minutia. It just cares about how it feels.

As you begin to entertain possibilities of what you might test, pay attention to the signals your body is sending you. Your body isn't going to lie to you, so if you list ten possible options and the thought of eight of them gives you a little pit in your stomach, don't blow that information off. Try the first two and see what happens.

WRITE THAT SH*T DOWN

Now that you have begun contemplating experiments and how they can help you gain clarity about your career, you're going to take a few steps to help you drill down even deeper on how you'd like to proceed during the experimentation phase.

Priming the Pump

Get out a blank piece of paper and hold it in the landscape position. On the top of the paper create four columns. Name them: About, Must Haves, Nice to Haves, No Way and No How Deal Breakers.

Next create eight rows underneath the About column and name them: Type of company/industry, Size of company, Salary, Culture/people, Room to grow, Working conditions, Location, and Job role/title.

This is your Job Assessment Chart. If you would prefer to download this chart you can go to www.careerswitch.org/charts.

Now, complete the chart as thoroughly as possible. Make clear distinctions between what you absolutely must have and what would be nice but not critical. Also, don't back down on your deal breakers. If you have a strong feeling about something, allow yourself to listen and act on behalf of it.

Design Your Experiment

Now, use the following four steps to design a job experiment that reflects the desires you put in your chart.

1. Make a list of the jobs you're curious about, ones you think you would be interested in doing. Refer back to the jobs you identified in Chapter 4 as well. Then search for job descriptions for each of the jobs. A good place to find some of these is Job-Descriptions.org. If you want to start your own business, research people who have started one. Remember the list of jobs you created in Chapter 4 and if you have any new ones to add, do so here.

2. Narrow down your list to your top two possibilities by asking yourself the following questions: Among all of the possibilities of what type of professional or entrepreneur I might become, which is most

interesting to me now? Which is easiest to test? Which make me most excited? Which create some anxiety for me?

3. Create a personal ad for your employment. In fifty words or less, describe yourself, explaining what's most awesome about you and why you would be the best person for the job. This is one of the most difficult writing assignments you can do. Writing short is not easy. Every word has to earn its right onto the page, and it has to do a job. Consider, what's the most important information the people in your desired industry need to know about you? When you are finished, put your job description somewhere that you can see it regularly. (I had mine on my laptop background screen for over a year.)

4. Identify people you know who work in the field or someone who would be a good person to talk to about it. If nobody comes to mind, then tell friends or colleagues what you're hoping to do and see if they could put you in touch with someone. Make coffee dates to talk to them about their work and then ask them if there is anyone else you should be talking to about it. Be a detective. Do your research.

Write a Letter to Doing

For this letter, I want you to stay in the moment and think specifically about the experiments you are going to do. Tell yourself what you want to do, what you want to get out of doing it, the kind of support you may need (and from whom), and what you hope to learn. What is your ideal scenario? Would you like to volunteer? Can you get an internship? Is there a project you really want to do at work that you can create a proposal for? Explain to Doing exactly what needs to happen and the steps you are going to take to make it happen. Then tell Doing what you want to get in return.

Play with It

Within the next week, if there is anyone you need to talk to about this idea, do so. If you have a spouse or a partner who will likely be impacted by your experiment, explain what you are doing and why you want to do it. Getting your partner and your kids on board is essential. They will likely have a lot of questions, especially if this idea is news to them. Give them some time to digest it, and be open with them. The more support you have from them, the more success you will have at getting what you need from the experiments.

Also within the next week, take your first step toward setting up your experiment. Call the hospital and talk to the volunteer coordinator, spend a day at the local cooking school, and talk to the students and instructors. Search for internships, search for part-time jobs, enroll in a course, create a proposal to work on a project, spend the day shadowing someone who does what you want to do, take someone out to lunch for an informational interview, or start doing the work on your own if that's possible.

The most important thing is to get your experiment started. By next week you should have a new "job." That job is to find out if you like doing what Passion suggested.

Write Two Letters to Passion

What you believe about passion matters. It matters because if you want to be passionate about your work, then you have to know what passion actually looks and feels like. Sometimes however what we think passion is about is not really what it's about. Let me explain. I have written many letters to Passion, and nearly always I was writing these letters in the desire stage of the Cycle of Complacency (Stage 1). I had a strong desire to do something, usually I thought it was writing, which I often confused with a passion for doing that writing, and I would write a letter to Passion describing what I wanted it all to look like. Then later, after I had experimented and tested and rejected and finally started actually doing the work I cared about, my letter to Passion sounded much different. That's okay. Writing a letter to Passion at any stage in your process is valuable because it's a way of keeping your hopes up, staying motivated, and keeping you in action.

Letter 1. Your first letter to Passion is best written before you begin all of your experiments. In this letter you are responding to a desire you have to reinvent your career or start something new and for that new work to be work you love. Explain what it would mean to you to be passionate about your work. How would you feel? What would you be doing? Who would you get to be if you were passionate about your work? How would your life change? What differences would the people in your life see? Why is having passion important to you?

This letter is designed to get you connected to a feeling you believe you're missing and it will also help you guide the direction of your experiments. If a possibility is presented to you but it's unlikely that all of the values you say are important to you will be met by doing that work, then maybe you should look for something else.

Letter 2. Your next letter to Passion is ideally written during or after the experimentation phase. (You can write additional ones at intervals, if you like.) In this letter you will be able to be more specific about what passion feels like and the surprises you've had while doing work you love so you can ask for more of it. For example, before I started doing work that I truly love I had some ideas of what I thought it would feel like to be passionate about my work, but they were just desired feelings. I didn't really know who I would become when I actually experienced them. Then one day after I dropped my daughter off at school I was heading home to do some work and I noticed how excited I was to get back. I couldn't stand being in the car because all I wanted to do was get back to work. I felt like someone had slipped me an upper, that's how high I was.

This was the first time that I had ever felt that way about work, so I thought about what it was specifically that I wanted to get back to. I knew that I wanted to keep creating situations where I felt this way. At this point I was starting to feel true passion about my work. With each day, my passion grew and grew and all I wanted to do was to find a way to sustain it. Writing the letters was one way and acting on behalf of them was another. I realized that once I started *doing,* my passion started speaking back to me in little ways every day. I thought my passion was writing, but it actually involved much more than that, something I only found out through experimenting.

Now I have a trifecta of letters that I write on a regular basis. My letter to Desire helps me get clear on what I want, my letter to Doing gives me direction to do what I want, and my letter to Passion drives me forward and keeps me on the path.

Debriefing the Experiments

Chances are it is going to take some time before you know if you would be a good fit for the work you're doing in your experiments. Although sometimes it only takes thirty minutes to know a job is not right. Regardless of your time-table, one of the best ways to evaluate an experiment and the job you're trying out is to ask yourself a series of questions designed to keep you focused on your goal and the change you're looking for. As I said earlier, sometimes emotions do all of the driving, especially when we're in such a bad place that we'd do anything to get out of our current job. These questions will help you to measure your experience in a more holistic way. Imagine working in this role full time for the next six months to a year, and then respond to the questions with "yes," "no," or "I don't know."

- Am I at my best when I am doing this work?

- Do I believe in the work, service, product, or organization?

- Am I being challenged?

- Is there great opportunity for growth and learning?

- Are the people I am working with "my people"? Are we a fit?

- Do I like the organizational style? Is it hierarchical or flat? Which do I like better?

- Am I able to use the best of me? Considering my best skills and talents, does this job make use of them?

- Are there people around me that I look up to who show an interest in my growth?

- Would I want to do my boss's job? Whose job would I want to do and does my current role put me on that path?

- How do I feel at the end of the day—energized, drained, excited for more, or can't wait to get out of there?

- What information am I missing or what more do I need to know to be able to evaluate this job more thoroughly?

For the questions to which you responded "no" or "don't know," go back to the chart you completed in the Priming the Pump exercise and see how they match up. For example, if you put great mentors as a "must have" but you responded "no" to questions 8 and 9, then that is a clue to pay attention. Between the questions and the chart, in addition to your emotions, you should be begin to get some good measures of whether or not any given role is a good fit. Having said that, just because you spend some time working in one HR department, it doesn't mean you know how all HR departments work. No two companies are alike. If you really thought HR was the place for you, but your first experiment was an utter disappointment, look for another opportunity in a different company. If after two or three experiments in different HR departments you find that you have not enjoyed any of them then at that point I might suggest going back and re-evaluating what it is you want. I would also recommend that you do some more interviews with people who work in HR so that you can bring some of the questions that came up as a result of your experiment to the table. The goal with the experiments is to first create momentum and then get information you can use to inform your next steps.

After you complete your letters and before you begin the next chapter, be sure to head over to www.Careerswitch.org/7review to get some more writing prompts and review what you've discovered so far.

Chapter 8
I Wrote a Letter to
Fear and It Told Me to Stop
Giving It So Much Airtime

"A life spent making mistakes is not only more honorable, but more useful than a life spent doing nothing."

—George Bernard Shaw

No book about change would be complete without a mention of the emotion of fear. I am going to talk about it because it is real and it's an emotion that prevents amazing, interesting, and creative people from doing work they are too scared to do. However, I want to make this discussion of fear short and sweet because, while some of our fears have basic survival value, the ones that usually get in the way of us changing careers or starting our own businesses are simply fears that are giving us information about our psychological status, and we have the power to either weaken or unlearn them. I chose to discuss fears at this point in the book because inevitably when I begin working with clients on getting their experiments started fears begin to show up and until they are able to move past them, the experiments don't get off the ground and they don't move forward and change careers. The great thing about fears however is that once we figure out how to counteract a fear, we can do it really quickly. I'm going to give you a tool to help you move through fear (if you have any) so you can get on with doing your crazy good work.

Note: I am not taking fears lightly. Some people have paralyzing and debilitating fears, and if you have a fear like that then I recommend you seek help from a specialist in this area as soon as possible. In this book I am address-ing minor fears that have major consequences, those we have the power to weaken and unlearn on our own.

All of us have five basic fears: the fears of extinction, mutilation, loss of autonomy, separation, and ego death. If you contemplate any of the fears you have, whether it's fear of rejection, fear of snakes, fear of imprisonment, or fear of not being worthy, they all fall under the umbrella of one of the five basic fears.

When we are confronted with something that makes us anxious, we antic-ipate an imagined experience and react in a reflexive way. The thing is, we are not reacting to the true fear, but rather to a micro-fear that represents the memories of fear. It happens so fast that we aren't even aware of it. For example, if you are not comfortable meeting new people, then when you open an invitation to a "meet and greet" event you will most likely turn down the invitation. You get caught up in the inner monologues you have about being uncomfortable in groups, and these ideas push you to reject those situ-ations. When you do this, you are reacting reflexively to an imagined experi-ence rather than accepting the anxiety simply as information whose hold on you needs to be weakened so that you can benefit from the party. Unless you change your perception and weaken the hold of the information on you, you take the anxiety as code for the real fear of separation or ego death and you shut yourself down.

So, what's the solution? How do you weaken or unlearn fears that have been keeping you from moving forward and changing careers? There are four steps to weakening a fear that's stopping you.

Step 1: View the Fear as Information

Most of our fears are not nearly as complicated as we think. In order to view a fear as information there are four questions you can ask yourself. Consider a fear that is stopping you from doing something right now. For example, let's say you have wanted to change your career and start your own business for years, but you've been too scared to take the first step. If we were working together one on one, here's how the inquiry might proceed.

"What is most important for you to do?" I would ask.

You would likely answer, "Get out of my current job and begin my own business doing X."

The next question I would ask would be: "How do you stop yourself from following through?"

Your answer may sound something like this: "I imagine my business failing or people telling me I am crazy or not being good enough or . . ."

My next question would be: "What do you do instead of finding a way out of your current job and starting your own business?"

You might say: "I complain about my job, I feel depressed, and I do a lot of thinking, but very little doing."

My final questions would be: "What if worrying that you might not be successful were no longer important to you? What if having the belief that you might fail were no longer important to you?"

Here's where you might begin to see how much you're holding yourself back and that you do have a choice. You might say, "If worrying if I was going to be successful were no longer important to me then I would spend my time moving forward on this. I would take the first step to start my business on the side. I would create a plan to leave my job in six months or a year. I would do what I really want instead of talking about it."

To give you an idea of how you might already be having similar conversations with yourself, here's a conversation I used to have with myself. The strong, audacious, bold, and fearless me and the scared, tentative, and safe me.

Strong: So, you want to be a writer?
Scared: Yes.
Strong: Really?
Scared: Yes, REALLY!
Strong: Because it seems to me that you might want something else?
Scared: Like what?
Strong: Like you want to go back to school for something you don't want to do. Like you want to keep working as a consultant on a topic you have zero

interest in. Like you want to hide behind other people who are doing their best work. Like maybe you just want to talk about writing.

Scared: I don't really want to do those things, but I *have* to.

Strong: Says who?

Scared: Says me.

Strong: Like I said, doing those other things are more important to you than writing.

Scared: No, they aren't, but I can't just write full time. I'll never make enough money.

Strong: Says who?

Scared: Says me. I've never made enough just writing to replace the money I make in my consulting work.

Strong: Oh. So you've tried? You really truly gave it your 100 percent and still nothing?

Scared: Well no, not exactly.

Strong: Not exactly what?

Scared: I haven't given 100 percent because I have so many other things I have to do that do make money or that help me create more potential for money that I have less time to devote to writing. I want it to be my full-time career, but for now it just has to be a small part of what I do.

Strong: So tell me this. Why do you keep distracting yourself with projects and potential instead of just taking all of that time and energy and putting it into your writing? All you have ever wanted to do since you picked up your first pencil was write. NOTHING is stopping you. Why are you stopping yourself? Why do you keep searching for your "thing" when it has been right under your nose for thirty-five years? You've already got your thing. You know it and everyone who has ever known you knows it. What are you doing?

Scared: Shit. This is it isn't it? The ugly truth. Okay, here it is. What if I fail? What if they hate me? What if I dump *everything* else into this career and just write and I'm not good enough? What if I have spent my entire life dreaming about something and secretly thinking it could be true, and then I don't have what it takes? Then I don't get to talk about "someday" anymore. My day came and I bombed. Then I'm back to zero.

Strong: Okay, back up. You've been writing for a living for twenty years. You've been paid good money to write. Maybe not as much as you make now, but you can do it, right?

Scared: Maybe.

Strong: All right then, let's cut the crap. Here's the only question that matters right now: What if creating all of these distractions (new projects, chasing after degrees, work you hate) was no longer important to you? What would get to happen for you then?

Scared: Those things aren't important to me!

Strong: Hell yes they are. It's easy to see what's important to you. Just look at what you spend your time doing.

Scared: Shit. You're right. But I'm scared.

Strong: Good. Now you're on to something. Again, what would get to happen if that fear that you won't be good enough was no longer important to you?

Scared: I would write a book. I would quit working for those clients. I would bring my writing business back to life. I would do the work I wanted instead of talking about it. I would explore the other parts of my career more vigorously too. I'd make them both work. I'd have the portfolio career I've always wanted but this time I would love all of the pieces of the pie, not just one.

This was a conversation I had with myself hundreds of times. Hundreds of times!

My mom jokes that I was born with a pencil in my right and a journal in my left. All I had ever wanted to do was find a way to write for money. Writing was what came easy to me. It's what I have always done in my free time, and even when I didn't have any free time. It's part of what makes me me, and when I would picture my life this is what I was always doing, and yet I would sabotage myself. When my writing business became too busy, I'd shut it down and stop taking clients, and the next thing I knew I was dreaming up some other business slant or partnership or taking on other marketing clients that would take me away from my writing and keep me safe. All in the name of fear.

It was wretched, debilitating, and uninspired.

Until one day I decided to look like a fool and not care. I decided that what people thought was no longer important to me and that the fear that was keeping me from doing what I wanted was no longer important to me. I quit working for clients I didn't love. I wrote a book. I began freelance writing again. I dug deeper into other career fields in order to balance my days. I chose doing over fearing and still nobody killed me or ate me.

Step 2: Remember that the Here and Now Is Your Best Defense

Fear comes in many forms (unease, worry, anxiety, dread, and so on) and the fear is always about something that *might* happen, but is not currently happening. Since you can only be right here, right now, but your mind is in the future, when you experience a fear you've actually created an anxiety gap that needs to be filled.

Fear is a construct of the mind that actually has a difficult time with the now time frame. It automatically imagines the future and, since its objective is to keep you safe (so nobody will kill you or eat you), it works overtime to make sure you do nothing to compromise your safety. So if you want to move forward, but your mind is intent on keeping you safe by encouraging inaction, what can you do? The best thing you can do is acknowledge your brain's intentions while reminding it that you have some pretty high intentions for yourself, and therefore, barring getting cornered by a hungry lion, you're going to accept the fear as its gift to you, but you're going to keep going anyway. You're even going to embrace it, as you'll see in Step 3.

Step 3: Include Fear as Part of the Experience

Uncertainty is part of the game of life. There is not a single person on this planet, no matter how successful, who does not face uncertainty. And not merely face it, but embrace it and thrive on it. When it comes to going after what we want, we have to include fear and uncertainty as part of the process, and embrace them as the driving forces that will propel us to depths we can't yet imagine. There is no other way.

Many people believe that it requires work, effort, and deep cognitive insight to release intense emotions like fear, and that by controlling our feelings, our thoughts, and our beliefs we will get "better." I don't agree. Rather I believe that we have a much better chance of freeing ourselves from uncomfortable feelings if we do nothing. When we do nothing about the thoughts or feelings that come into our experience, we actually eliminate our reactive responses and, as a consequence, stop judging the thoughts to be good or bad.

When something is no longer good or bad it loses its charge and we lose our attachment to it. In doing this, we create the space for the problem or the challenge to run its course. We don't try to head it off at the pass, cut it off, or throw it out of the car. We don't try to quash the fear or ignore it or try and find our way around it. We include it and we let it coast to its natural resting place, which inevitably allows it to dissolve.

When a fear shows up, my advice is to do nothing. Simply notice it, rather than reacting against it or actively trying to resist it. Give it a place to live in you. It only receives a charge if you give it a charge. You can even have a little fun with it, which you'll see in Step 4.

Step 4: Express Gratitude for the Fear, but Tell It You Are Way Too Busy to Let It Control the Show

I know it may sound a little woo woo, or maybe even crazy, to express gratitude for your fear, but that's exactly what I suggest you do. One of the values of seeing fear as simply another piece of information is that you realize how lucky you are to be able to get the other side of the story. Your fear is like a good, but highly risk adverse friend playing devil's advocate for you, which makes it far easier to say no to it.

Let me explain by going back to the original example we looked at in which you want to leave your job and start your own business. Let's pretend you sit down to coffee with your very rational and risk adverse friend to fill her in on what you've been considering. You lay out your plan for leaving your job and starting your own business over the next six months. Being the kind of friend who checks the stove three times before she leaves the house, she gets a little nervous about your idea. She thinks it sounds great, but she can't see how you are going to make it happen, and she's having a really hard time faking her enthusiasm and encouragement. So you ask her what she thinks and she says everything you've already said to yourself such as, "What if it doesn't work? How's your husband going to respond? How could you leave a good job with benefits for such an unsure thing?"

Now, chances are that when a friend starts poking holes in your plan you're going to defend it like your life depended on it. You will say something like, "I understand what you're saying, but I've been thinking about this for a long time and I know what I have to do. It's going to be hard, but I can do this." Well, that's exactly the same approach you should take with your inner voice of fear.

Your fear means as well as a good friend. It's only trying to keep you safe. But just because it has great intentions doesn't mean its advice is right for you in *this* moment. So, when you start to take steps toward starting your own business and fear shows up and your anxious inner monologue starts warning you that you might not be good enough to make your plan happen, say, "Thank you for sharing. I know you mean well, but I have a few tricks up my sleeve that you know nothing about. I appreciate it, but I've got this."

Being able to be playful with fear may not be something that happens for you overnight, but having this tool available will help you become far more aware than you have ever been about the little micro-fears that encourage inaction. You will notice them more regularly, and each time they show up you will give them less airtime. You will learn to distance your experience in the here and now from the vision of a mind intent on imagining a negative future that may feel real, but does not exist. It will get easier and easier to embrace your fears like you would the advice of a well-intentioned friend, and carry them with you as move toward your dreams.

Fear Mitigation

Before we move on to the writing exercises, I want to take this opportunity to do some fear mitigation. I want to set you up for success by helping you anticipate the bumps in the road so you can get past them and cruise through.

As you take the steps to switch your career, rejoin the workforce, or start a business, or even experiment as you've started to do, it's likely that you're going to feel fear at various points along the road. That fear will immediately turn into language designed to keep you exactly where you are. I know you aren't going to be okay with that, so neither am I.

Here's a list of the most common fears my clients have come to me with over the years and some statements you can make (or questions you can ask yourself) to help you include the fear in your plans and still move on to accomplish your big goals.

Fear: I won't make enough money. Says who? *Exactly* how much money do you need? Why do you need it? Are *all* of your needs more important than you doing work you love? What research do you have that proves you will not make enough money? What if you made at least half of what you need? Could you make the other half doing something else?

Fear: My family will think I'm crazy. Does that make them right? Can you recall any other time in your life when you wanted to do something and someone else thought you were crazy for doing it? What happened? Five years from now would you rather be someone who didn't listen and went for it or someone who let someone else decide what was best for him or her?

Fear: I'm not good enough. You're right. Nobody is. Once you realize this, you'll stop allowing it to be an excuse for not doing what you secretly want. Worrying about being good enough is a self-indulgent time killer. Don't worry about being good enough; just go be crazy great at something you love.

Fear: I'll get rejected. Get in line. Rejection is the Universe's way of telling you there is something better for you. Rejection is not a personal attack; it is information you can use to help you move closer to your goals.

Fear: I'll have to go backwards – go to the bottom of the ladder. Your life is not a ladder, so stop worrying about whether you are going up or down. If you take a step, the only place you are going is forward. Taking a step invites learning, experience, and knowledge. You get to define what rung you are on.

Fear: I don't have a strong enough network. Get one. Lots of people have one. You are not so special or "so" unique that you cannot have one, too. It's not easy to build one if you don't like to network, market yourself, meet new people, and so on. Should that matter? Who said anything about it being easy? You want something great, right? Then you have to be great first.

Fear: Nobody would ever hire me. I've been out of the workforce for too long. Show me the proof. If you don't have any, find some.

Fear: I'll make the wrong decision. Maybe you will. What's the worst that could happen if you do? If that happened, what would you do then? All "wrong" decisions give you valuable information. Imagine what you could do with that instead.

Fear: I don't know anything about business. It might fail. It might. Many do. If you don't know anything about it, learn. Study. Find a mentor. Is holding the thought that it might fail more important to you than starting and running a successful business? If not, then you have no business getting caught in the worry stage. Take steps first, and then decide if you have reason to worry.

With this list in mind I want to make clear that not all fears related to experimenting or career change are nonsense. If, for instance, you have a fear of not making enough money, it's absolutely possible that it is a justifiable fear: You may not able to do what you want full time and make enough money to support your family. However, if all you have is the fear, but you have no solid evidence to show you that what you imagine in the future is true, then you still have some work to do. This process is not about ignoring all of the signals we get or the fears we feel. This is about not letting them stop us so much that we fail to take the steps we need to get the kind of information we need to make a good decision.

WRITE THAT SH*T DOWN

Most of the time we let our fears drive our behavior and we don't even realize we're allowing that to happen. In this section you're going to declare what you want and then what you're going to do to move through the fear that's been stopping you so you can achieve it.

Priming the Pump

For this exercise you're going to walk through the example I gave you at the beginning of the chapter, but this time you're going to focus on your own fears. Take out your journal and write the answers to the following questions:

- What is the most important thing you want to do?
- How do you stop yourself from following through on X?
- What do you do instead of doing X?
- What if worrying that Y might happen was no longer important to you?
- What if having the belief that Z was no longer important to you? What would get to happen for you then? What would your career look like then?

Write a Letter to Fear

Now that you have anticipated common fears and the language of those fears, identified what is stopping you from doing what you want and acknowledged what would get to happen for you if X, Y, and Z were no longer important to you, it's time to write a letter to Fear. What do you want to tell it? What does it need to know about you? What are you going to do the next time it shows up? What have been the consequences in the past of listening to Fear, and what are you going to do to make sure that the next time you feel afraid it will be a positive experience?

When I wrote this letter originally, I noticed that I had three major fears that were showing up over and over again and causing significantly negative results. I also realized that they were so common that each time they showed up I quickly accepted them as true. I had taken them on as if they were genetic characteristics rather than as bits of information I could actually do something with.

Once I wrote the letter I received a powerful message: "Stop giving your fears so much airtime. You're wasting your time on things that aren't true." So that's what I did—and what you'll do, too, when you put all of this into practice.

Play with It

One of the qualities you need to have to overcome fears is courage, so that's what you're going to practice today. Consider something you've wanted to do as it relates to your career that is relatively low risk. I'm not suggesting you make it low risk, because I don't believe you're ready to go full out and make some huge changes right now, but rather because I know that once you take a little risk and discover that the terrible, awful, and irreversible things that your mind convinced you might happen actually didn't happen, then you will move even more quickly to up the ante.

Maybe you want to start your own business, but don't know where to start, and you're afraid of looking stupid so you've done nothing. Today I want you to reach out by phone or email to someone who is doing the kind of work you want to do and interview them. If you don't know of anyone doing what you want then contact someone who started a similar business and invite them to join you for coffee or to do a Skype video chat. Explain your situation and tell them what you're looking for. If they say no, which I highly doubt, then find someone else. Stop letting the fear of looking stupid get in the way of your goal.

Maybe in order to have the career you really want you are going to need to go back to school, but you've hesitated to take the first step because you're scared you won't get in, or that even if you do get in then you'll never get a good job, so you spend a huge chunk of time researching training programs and letting it all stop there. Contact the department and let the staff know that you are considering returning to school. Tell them you would like to meet with an admissions advisor and a member of the faculty so you can learn more about the process and the program.

Maybe you know that if you want to make a career change getting out and making connections with people is your best option for growing a relevant network, but you are really uncomfortable meeting new people. You're afraid of rejection and worry that nobody will talk to you or you won't know what to say. Accept that you will probably feel uncomfortable, but don't let that be more important than connecting with people who you might be able to help and who might be able to help you. If it will make it easier, enlist the help of an outgoing friend who would be willing to go with you and show you how it's done. Or find someone who specializes in helping people make connections and learn a process that will help you feel more comfortable at the meeting.

Another great way to feel more at ease is to contact the host or hostess of the event and see if you can volunteer. I get out of sorts if I am left to randomly mingle in large groups so I always try to land myself a job. I have offered to plan and host MeetUps, greet people at the door with meeting materials, and I even plopped myself in front of a snow cone maker at my daughter's friend's birthday party once so I could interact with everyone who came through the line! People love to talk to those who are "in the know," and even when I get a question like "Where's the bathroom?" it inevitably turns into something more.

There are a lot of ways to make these situations more comfortable. Find a way that would make it as comfortable as possible for you and make an appointment to attend a networking coffee or a MeetUp or an event this week.

Whenever I am scared to do something and I have been fretting about it for too long, my friend Sandy always says to me, "It's not like they are going to kill you and eat you."

How can you argue with that?

After you complete your letters and before you begin the next chapter, be sure to head over to www.careerswitch.org/8review to get some more writing prompts and review what you've discovered so far.

Chapter 9
I Wrote a Letter to Death and My Voice Wrote Me Back

"Her voice changed like a bird's:
There grew more of the music, and less of the words."

—Robert Browning

I used to think about death a lot. I worried about dying. I worried about the people I love dying. And even though I was only in my early thirties I had this fixation on death. I felt like my time was running out and all the good times and exciting experiences were behind me. Now I know that my obsession was all a product of being in a bad marriage where I felt like I was dying inside a little bit every day. When I left that marriage my emotional state improved dramatically and instead of believing the best was behind me I felt sure the best was yet to come. Then it happened again when I was working with that troublesome client I mentioned earlier. I felt myself losing my confidence again, losing my voice, and feeling like my possibilities were limited.

In an attempt to start finding my voice, I began working on a project that was the most meaningful work I'd ever done. One of my uncles, who had been a huge part of my life since the day I was born, was deteriorating quickly from ALS and I was going to write his memoir. He wasn't just my uncle, but a person who impacted thousands of peoples' lives with his work, his philanthropy, his love, his generosity, both spiritually and financially, and I wanted to preserve that history for my family and everyone else who knew him. It was a bittersweet project, because the idea of sitting down with him to record his life and the lessons he had learned was going to be a beautiful experience.

At the same time knowing that pretty soon this memoir would be all I had left of him was nearly too much to bear.

I sat down and sketched out the entire book for my uncle. I compiled all of the questions I wanted to ask him and made a plan for how we would get our interviews done. He was going to sell his part of a law firm, and then we'd have time to work.

He died two months later.

Not six months after that, one of my other uncles, his brother, passed away from another insidious disease. It felt like a dirty joke. These two men who only two years before had been strong and vivacious, succumbed to horrible diseases that ravaged their bodies and minds to the point that they were shells of their former selves. These two men were wildly successful entrepreneurs and philanthropists who had made a significant impact in their family and community. They lived big, full lives, and they made what seemed impossible happen for themselves and others and because of that I had looked up to them my whole life. As I sat in a coffee shop one morning before one of their funerals, for the first time in a really long time I connected with my voice again and reminded myself that while I am on this planet I had better make good use of it.

It's a cliché, of course, that when we lose someone we've loved deeply we finally see how precious time is. But when death knocks on the doors of two people you love within six months of each other this feeling is magnified by a factor of one thousand. Add to that the fact that both these men did work that brought them an immeasurable amount of joy and allowed them the spiritual and financial freedom to give to others in a profound way and you can see why I was more motivated than ever to use everything I had been given while I was still able to do so.

When we have the chance to reinvent ourselves we have an obligation to ourselves and those around us to go big. To take everything we know about conventional jobs and career paths and toss them in favor of the wildest thing we can imagine. I know that's not always easy to do. When we start to think about what is possible for us we often experience cognitive dissonance, the discomfort of holding conflicting ideas, beliefs, and values at the same time. For example, messages about what you should do and what you're capable of doing may have been so strong while you were growing up that all the new beliefs you're starting to have about what's possible may be difficult to reconcile. You feel torn and when faced with an opportunity one part of you is saying, "Hell yes. I can do this!" and the other part of you is saying, "Who do you think you are? Don't even try it."

The goal then is to create a new movement that you can get behind so that whenever the voice inside of you starts ranting on about why you should be choosing what is practical and possible rather than what seems crazy and unreasonable you will be strong in your response. Mine is called *Melani's Movement* primarily because I wasn't feeling very creative on the day I decided I needed my own movement. Nonetheless, I knew I had to name it something because then if I chose to go against it, it would feel really big. Naming it has helped me keep myself in check.

Here are the principles that guide my movement.

- What you do for work is far less important than *how* you do it.

- When you align your work with your values you will sleep well.

- Find your gift, your love, and your skill, and then use them up until you take your final breath. Leave nothing behind.

- Stop doing things that keep you in rehearsal. Do not spend time learning unless you intend to spend time doing something with the knowledge.

- Give far more than you take.

- Take every opportunity you have to share your gift with others. Whether your gift is time, money, advice, or a special skill, give it generously wherever it is needed and you will never feel empty.

- Doing is more powerful than imagining. (That's because what's possible for us is nearly always more than what we can imagine in our minds. When we *do* more than we *think* we'll be surprised on a regular basis by what we're capable of.)

Those principles guide all of the decisions I make about my work and career. Without them it would be easy to get taken off track, go down unproductive rabbit holes and lose my voice, something I have promised I'll never let happen again. Does that mean that I would never take a job or work that I don't love because I have bills to pay? No. It simply means that those principles are my lighthouse, guiding me to what's right for me and what's in alignment with my values.

WRITE THAT SH*T DOWN

What's your movement? In this section you'll get to name it and identify its guiding principles.

Priming the Pump

Now it's time to give your voice a name and start your own movement. Take out your journal and respond to the following questions:

- What is the name of your movement?
- What are the principles that are going to guide your movement? Consider people you admire, your own life experience and lessons you've learned on this career clarity journey in choosing the principles that will guide you.
- What is most important to you and what factors do you need to remind yourself of when it's time to make decisions about your career?

Write a Letter to Your Voice

Most of us, at some point or another have lost our voice or have allowed it to become quieter relative to all of the other voices we hear in our lives. If you have been in a job that's been draining you or you've felt unfulfilled from not working, then it's possible that you've spent time not being honest with others about what you really want or not being honest with yourself because you're unsure if what you want is even possible. Your doubts can cause you to hold back. If you want to get clarity on your career, your voice needs to be strong and unencumbered and you have to be willing to put yourself, your ideas, and your beliefs out there in a bold way.

In this letter you're going to see what it's like to use your voice. Imagine that you have an audience of 1,000 people. These can be any 1,000 people you want. Maybe they are people who work in the industry you'd like to work in, maybe they're your family members, or maybe they're your future fans. Imagine you have fifteen minutes in front of these people and during that time you get to share a culmination of all you've been discovering about yourself since you started "writing that sh*t down". This is your chance to make your case loud and clear about what you want, why you want it, and most importantly, why you are the perfect person to make it happen, whatever "it" may be.

When one of my clients wrote this letter, she said that when she sat down to write it in her journal she was as nervous as she would have been if she were actually speaking in front of a big audience. She even tried to write it two other times before she was able to "handle it." She said,

So far a lot of this work has been low risk. The experiment I am doing even feels pretty low risk because I am just volunteering and therefore people's expectations of me are not as high. But now that I have to put into words what I want and why I want it and why they should hire me, I feel the doubts creeping in and even I am questioning myself. I need to write the letter again because I am pretty sure even I would not hire myself with that act but this has been invaluable in helping me articulate what I am trying to do. I am even clearer now than I was before I wrote the letter."

When you want to switch careers, more often than not you're going to have to make a case for why you're doing it and why your prospective employer would want to take a chance on you. Even if you're starting your own business, this is true. Entrepreneurs often have to make a case to prospective clients or to bankers who want to know they are a good bet and safe investment. This is a great, low risk way to practice doing it and hopefully someday soon you will actually have an opportunity to make your case to someone who can help you get exactly what you wrote in your letter.

Play with It

Read your letter to an audience of one. Instead of 1,000 people, pick one person and ask her if she would be willing to listen to your letter and offer you some feedback. It's critical that you say it out loud to her rather than having her read it. Explain the goal: that you are trying to get clarity on what you want, why you want it, and why you are the person to do it. Also, let her know that your ability to communicate this clearly, strongly and effectively is critical, so any feedback on your tone, language, and style would be appreciated.

When a friend did this for me it was a profoundly important experience. I went into it feeling sure of myself, cocky even, that I knew what I wanted and how I wanted it all to play out. I also felt sure she'd find no holes in my argument. By the end it felt like she found nothing but holes. Reading my letter out loud to someone who had no investment in which career paths I chose, but who had tremendous insight to me as a person, helped me to reshape my path into something that excited me even more.

This sounds a little bit like homework and it may seem less fun than some of the other activities I've asked you to do, but I promise that doing this is a great way to find out where you are in the process of gaining clarity, and, if you discover you're less clear than you thought you were, I recommend taking time at this point to go back through the book and see if you can identify any spot you may have rushed through or an activity you did that you thought you were finished with. See if it may need a little more time and attention. One of my clients who was interested in working in human resources wrote her letter and she realized that she was having a hard time explaining exactly what she wanted to do and why she would be perfect for the job because she didn't have enough information about Human Resources work, her field of interest. She therefore went back to the chapter on experiments and decided to interview two more people and shadow someone to see what his day really looked like.

These actions led her to some more experiments, which greatly informed her letter and more importantly, her next steps.

Keep checking in with yourself throughout this process to make sure you're getting what you wanted. The goal of this book is to help you get clarity on what you want to do. It may not happen over night, but if you stick with it, it will happen.

After you complete your letters and before you begin the next chapter, be sure to head over to www.careerswitch.org/9review to get some more writing prompts and review what you've discovered so far.

Chapter 10
I Wrote a Letter to Reinvention and My Mojo Wrote Me Back

"Enjoy yourself. It's later than you think."

—Chinese Proverb

When I asked my clients to describe what it felt like for them to undergo the process of achieving clarity on their careers, here's what some said: It was messy, crazy, raw, unpredictable, uncomfortable, maddening, exciting, frustrating, and freeing.

Seeking clarity can be all of those things and more, so I want to share my top eleven recommendations for bringing out your mojo during what has the potential to be a messy process. You'll need your mojo now more than ever to keep your cool when progress is slow, to stick with it when you feel like you're swimming upstream, to not get taken out when fear creeps in and to keep moving forward when it would be faster and easier to go back to the devil you know.

> Mojo = Self-confidence, self-assuredness, chutzpa, charm, magnetism, resilience, gumption

Recommendation 1: Play

If you're able to approach this process of achieving clarity on your next steps in a fun and playful way then you will have taken away its power to be scary. There are so many chances to make this fun. I had such a great time whenever I sat down to write my letters that I forgot about being stressed or anxious. When I was volunteering and interviewing I felt like I was the luckiest person in the room, getting the access without having to make the commitment. Most of all, by approaching this as an adventurous fact-finding mission, I was able to take myself and the entire situation less seriously. I am not minimizing how stressful it can be when you are working in a job you hate and are desperate for quick change, or when you have been laid off and you need clarity fast because the money is running out; however, all of this work has to get done so you might as well have fun while you're doing it.

Recommendation 2: Be a Beginner

There's a concept in Zen practice called *beginner's mind*. The beginner's mind refers to having an attitude of openness and lack of preconceptions when you are studying or learning something new. When you approach something with a beginner's mind you are free of the idea of knowing something already or having heard something before. All that exists is the possibility of something new, something never before heard, seen, or experienced.

Most of the time when we take in information during a conversation, we have thoughts going on in our head about what's being said. For example, as it relates to changing careers, you may choose to interview someone and even though you approach the interview with the best of intentions, and you are taking diligent notes on what your subject is saying to you, you are automatically interpreting what you hear, and so write that down, while skipping the rest of the information being offered. You might even have come up with your version of what *you* think is important for the person to say to you before the interview starts, and then not be open to hearing alternative answers to your questions. You're checking out of the moment by holding on to preconceptions.

Instead of thinking about how what you are hearing does or does not fit with what you already know or what you think is going to be true, focus on listening. Take it all in with the beginner's mind. This will allow you to pick up on nuances you would otherwise miss, and in doing so learn even more clues that will ultimately lead to the clarity you seek.

Recommendation 3: Be Prepared for the Heavy Lifting

Writing all of your sh*t down may be a fun and playful activity, but acting on behalf of the ideas that arose while you were writing can be anything but. Getting clarity is an ongoing process. One minute you'll feel like you've nailed it, and thirty minutes later you're sure you have it all wrong. You have to be prepared for anything to happen, and be willing to keep going no matter what. As we talked about in Chapter 6, creating a sense of urgency even when it's difficult and you doubt your every move is what is going to launch you out of the Cycle of Complacency and onto the Wave of Change.

If you expect gaining clarity to require a lot of effort on your part, then there's less of a chance that you'll get taken out by the process. Then when you move from trying to find clarity to trying to find your dream job or trying to start your own business in the next phase of career reinvention, you'll be ready for it.

Recommendation 4: Master the Art of the Detour

When I was a history teacher I used to spend hours and hours planning each lesson down to the very last detail. My teacher friends would ask me why I would spend so much time on planning when most of the time my lessons never played out even remotely as I planned them. My answer: "The more structured I am, the more flexible I can be."

I found that the more detailed my plan was the easier it was to veer off course, change on the fly, and have fun with it. The same holds true for changing careers. I have yet to coach someone through a career change where the process unfolded exactly how they had planned. Mine sure didn't. Even so, the more work my clients do when it comes to researching jobs, interviewing experts, doing experiments, and going down the path "as if" it were already real, the easier it has been for them to face their career detours with a positive mindset and have fun with them.

Detours, such as having to stay in your job longer than you planned because your new idea doesn't have financial legs yet, or starting down one path and realizing it's not the right fit for you, are signs that you should be paying attention. Like fears, they may be frustrating, but each time you're faced with one, consider that it's probably giving you information that's essential to your search.

Recommendation 5: Leave Your Old Identity Without Losing Your Legitimacy

Oftentimes, when you want to make a radical change you want to leave the past as far behind as you can. And when you're trying to find some level of clarity, which can be a multilayered process, it can be freeing to let the past go. It's challenging to straddle the line between the old and the new, but even though the idea of bringing your former identity along with you as you pursue brand-new dreams and goals may sound heavy and uninteresting, you want to be careful not to throw out the good with the bad.

I made that mistake myself when I was so miserable in my old role doing marketing that I deleted my blogs and erased every trace I could of myself online in that capacity when I gave it up. It was liberating and exciting to say goodbye to that life and it was a profound symbolic gesture towards welcoming back my old business as a writer, but I also erased a lot of content and credibility that would have gone a long way to helping me rebuild my freelance writing business more quickly.

You are the sum of every job you've had, every decision you've made, and every experience you've been lucky enough to have. Bring those parts of you to the process of finding clarity and your next career role. Don't be afraid to tell someone about how your achievements in one field will translate to achievements in another, no matter how disparate the two fields may appear to be. Gone are the days where people stayed in one job or one career for their entire lives. It is expected for people to change and grow on a regular basis.

I used to be ashamed of my career hopping. Now I embrace it. I hope you will embrace *everything* you bring to the table, too.

Recommendation 6: Speak up

On the road to clarity, you may be tempted to keep a tight lip on your plans until total clarity comes knocking on your door. You may be unsure of yourself in the midst of all of your questioning and researching, and you may even feel a little bit vulnerable. That's natural, but speaking up about what you are trying to accomplish may be the best thing you can do. The more people who know what you are up to, the more people will be looking out for you and doing what they can to help you achieve your goals.

Some of my clients have chosen to send emails to a few of their closest friends and family telling them they are considering a change and giving them a list of a few paths they are considering. Some of my clients have sent out a similar email to their entire list of contacts. Both camps have had huge success from doing so. When you need help with something as complex as a career change, you need to get on people's radar so that the next time your friends go to a party and meet someone who does exactly what you want to do they immediately make a note to put you two in touch.

When you're willing to involve other people, and let them help you, you'll be able to find clarity much more quickly than if you were content to try and do all of this on your own. If getting clarity on what you want to do next is truly a priority for you then it will be far more important for you to speak up than to stay quiet.

Recommendation 7: Own Your Superhero-ness

Superheroes are not all created equal. Some have extraordinary physical power, some have mastered a specific skill, and still others use weapons or technology to accomplish whatever crazy obstacle they face. When we hear the word "superhero" most of us quickly imagine colorful capes and masks, especially tight tights, and a whole mess of accoutrements that quite frankly do not look sexy on anybody. Still, we can all agree that superheroes possess extraordinary powers and abilities, and they use these to benefit others without expecting anything in return.

If attendance at Comic-Con and the blockbuster movies that people flock to are evidence of our feelings, we love the superhero. We are inspired by their motivation to serve at all costs, to continue to battle the same enemy over and over, to help the little guys, to be able to happily and comfortably survive on no visible means of income, and to nearly always come out unscathed at the end.

In fact, we love the story so much that we believe it. The problem is that we believe that's a job for someone else. Not true. Furthermore, the only way you're going to be able to reinvent your career and come out on top is to embrace your own Superhero-ness.

Allow me to introduce you to your personal superhero. Go to the nearest bedroom in your house and grab a sheet. Pull it off the bed, tie it around your neck, and look in the mirror. Meet your superhero. How does that feel? Strike a pose. Take a picture. Post it above your desk on your bulletin board where you can see it every day.

If you want to create a crazy good career for yourself, you have to be the superhero of your own life. You have to be willing to take some hard knocks and keep going no matter how impossible the tasks on the road may appear. You have to believe in yourself like Superman believed he could save Lois Lane and Wonder Woman knew she could tear steel doors off their hinges and run 60 M.P.H., because when everything feels difficult and slow and uncomfortable and uncertain, your *belief* in your ability to keep going and succeed is the only thing strong enough to get you where you want to go.

Go play around in your superhero costume for a while and see how it feels. Then, whenever you find yourself going down the path of "I can't do this, it's too hard," pull out that cape and be the superhero you were born to be.

Recommendation 8: Feed Your Body

Did you know that your body tells a story?

Consider this: How does the story you tell change when one or more of the following are true?

- You are tired and weak
- You have low blood sugar

- You have high blood sugar
- You have a stomachache
- You have a headache
- You are in pain
- You have insomnia
- You are sedentary

It changes a lot, right? Even a slight decrease in blood sugar changes your emotional, mental, and spiritual state.

Consider this: Have you ever found yourself contemplating a serious life issue, such as leaving your husband, quitting your job, or moving, when you were really tired? What happens? Most likely your emotional state is compromised—things seem better or much worse than they really are. You may find that you speak in superlatives, see no hope, feel defeated, and are too exhausted to make sense. That's because when your physical state changes, everything becomes colored. Your emotional, mental, and spiritual states need nourishment as much as your physical body. Without proper rest, nutrition, and exercise, they all suffer.

The body was built to last, certainly. We are strong creatures from the get go. However, if we want to achieve something utterly extraordinary in our lives—and in our careers—we have to invest the bodies we were given with extraordinary energy.

More rest, better nutrition, and exercise—delivered consistently, predictably, and enduringly—will dramatically improve not only your physical health and well-being, but your mental, emotional, and spiritual states. Where there is a harmony between body, mind, and spirit, what you do, your calling or mission becomes the means to experience a personal potential greater than can be achieved by your mind alone.

Consider this. In their book *The Psychic Side of Sports*, Michael Murphy and Rhea A. White make it clear that when we push against our psychobiological limits, the brain tissues record a remarkable range of mystical pleasures, such as extraordinary inner vision, peace, stillness, calm, detachment, freedom, floating, ecstasy, power, control, unity, mystery, and awe.[1] These are just a few of the psychic rewards of sport, of using your body and pushing your body to its limits.

Being physical every day does more than make you feel better and keep your heart and other organs healthy, it feeds your soul and your mind in a way you cannot do by simply burying yourself in work. With physical work comes more creative problem solving, more innovation, better relationships, and so much more you couldn't possibly predict, all things you need in great supply when you embark on a career change.

Your body holds so many clues to what's going on in your life at any given time. Use your body and the clues it gives you to navigate the rough waters of career reinvention. The great thing about your body is that it doesn't lie.

Recommendation 9: Give It Time

"Am I there yet? Am I there yet?" I say it all the time when it comes to my career. I can be as annoying as a six-year old boy on a cross-country road trip. The only difference is that I don't say it out loud.

When it comes to achieving clarity on how to reinvent your career, most people want change to happen now (or yesterday, ideally), but it doesn't work that way. Like I say to my daughter and my dad said to me, "It's going to take as long as it takes." When my clients ask me, "How long do you think it will take?" I hate what comes next. I hate that I have to tell them that it takes time because that's the one thing that people who come to me are certain they don't have. But as long as you're living and breathing and entertaining the question "What's next for my career?" you have time, and as long as each step you take brings you more clarity, then you are on the right path.

If you're feeling terribly impatient, remember, you can always write a letter to Time and ask it, "What more do I need to learn?" or "What is the waiting teaching me?"

Recommendation 10: Remember, It's Only Big Because You Haven't Done It Yet

During a trip I once took to an event, I arrived at the hotel and my room wasn't ready. To kill some time I decided to do something I hate doing even more than waiting: head to the mall. I didn't have a car so I had to run there, seven miles each way. As I was heading out, the doorman asked me where I was running. I told him to the mall. He thought I was crazy. When I showed up a few hours later, sweaty, tired, and bright red from the blazing sun, he had a list of questions: "Do you run a lot? Are you tired? How long have you been running?" He was genuinely interested and even a bit overwhelmed that it didn't seem like that big of a deal to me.

So, how does something like that become easy?

In contemplating this question I thought about all of the goals I have accomplished that I take for granted and those that I do on a daily basis that are second nature to me. Then I thought about the things that scare me, the things that I think about doing or wish I were doing and how they create a bit of anxiety for me. That led me to realize something great: Most of the things I want to do only seem big because I haven't done them *yet*.

There was a time when I first started distance running in high school that a marathon seemed huge, when getting paid really well to do work I love (while in my pajamas) was out of reach, when earning two master's degrees and getting great funding for Ph.D. programs (which I didn't accept) to study what I loved seemed like a big deal. Once each of those things ultimately happened, it no longer felt big.

The dream you have right now for your work and your career may seem big, or like a dream better dreamed by a special few, but that's only because you haven't reached it yet. Whether it's a specific position you want to land, an amount of money you want to command for your services, or a position of power you want to achieve, it's not too big for you. It only feels that way because you haven't done it yet. There will always be the thing that seems big to us. That's what drives us, keeps us on track, and inspires us to do more and be more every day.

The challenge is in not letting what feels too big take you out. As you navigate your career reinvention, keep that truth in mind.

Recommendation 11: Do, Make, and Give What Feels Good

The fact that you have come this far tells me that you're ready for change. Continuing to do what you have been doing is not going to work anymore. So, now that you have opened yourself up to a world of new possibilities, make sure that your choice leads you to places that will let you do, make, and give what feels good. At the end of the day, how you feel matters. It makes no sense to embark on a dramatic career change and not demand something better on the other side.

Just as I gave you a list of questions in Chapter 5 to help you measure how good of a fit each experiment was for you, another question you need to answer throughout the entire career switch process is this: Is what I am doing, making, or giving making me feel good? If the answer is yes, keep moving forward. If the answer is no, go back and find the gap between what you value and the work you're doing.

WRITE THAT SH*T DOWN

One of the best ways to help you keep your hopes up as you go through this process is to create your own reinvention story, which is what you're going to do next.

Priming the Pump

Take out your journal and respond to the following questions.

1. Out of the eleven recommendations I gave you, what are two that you need the most help with right now?

2. What can you do to get support around them?
3. On a scale of 1–10, how much clarity do you have around what's next for your career? If you are not at a 10, what would help you get there?

Write a Letter to Your Reinvention

The first step of career reinvention is getting clarity on what you want to do, a process I have shared with you in this book. While we are not going to get into the next phase of career reinvention, which is finding a job, there is a tremendous amount of value in writing your own career reinvention story before you even take that step. So that's what you're going to do next. First, however, I'd like you take thirty-seven minutes to watch *The Lemonade Movie,* if you haven't already seen it. (You can find it at LemonadeMovie. com.) This is one of my favorite collections of stories about people who were laid off and then reinvented themselves in surprising and heartwarming ways. It will inspire, motivate, and likely give you even more ideas for how you'd like your story to play out.

Go.

Now that you've seen the movie, get ready to write your letter to Reinvention. In this letter, begin by telling Reinvention everything you've learned, what you are and are not clear about, and what you're excited about as you imagine taking your next step in the process toward the career that makes your heart sing.

Next, write your story of how you want it to go. Imagine that your favorite magazine has asked you to share your story of how you went from working in a job that drained you to doing work that lights you up. You get to decide how it goes. How might you use your story to inspire others?

Every other letter you have written to this point has been more in the moment and real, so this exercise may feel a little bit airy-fairy. Do it even if you're reluctant. There is incredible power in writing your own story. Partly because when you write down how you want something to play out you can connect it to images in your mind, which is exactly the kind of suggestion you need. Also, if you aren't clear on the story you want to be able to tell someone else, you might miss some of the important pieces you'll need along the way to make it happen. Identifying those pieces will give you confidence.

Write your letter. Hold nothing back and allow yourself to have it the way you want it. When you see yourself on paper, just like people would if they were reading your article someday in their favorite magazine, you'll think you've got a black belt in awesome . . . and you'll be right.

Play with It

Now that you have spent some time on Fantasy Island it's time to turn the story you wrote into something practical you can do right now.

1. Go through the story and make a list of all of the items in it that require action on your part. For example, one of my clients' desires was to become the national expert on résumé writing. In her reinvention story, she had written about being on the news and giving advice on a live TV segment. At the time she had no contacts in the media, so an obvious step for her to take was to begin watching career segments more closely and establishing relationships with the local reporters who reported on career-related issues. Her goal was to establish herself locally and then move into national markets. In writing this story, she was able to deconstruct what she would need to do to make that happen.

   Likewise, after I wrote my letter to Reinvention, I had a list of over twenty-five actions I knew I would have to take to make my career dream come true.

2. Now that you have your action list, identify three items you will take action on this week. You don't have to complete them fully at this point, but do keep your eye on them to ensure that you'll make progress. Keep your complete list accessible so you keep what needs to happen in your line of sight at all times.

Chapter 11
I Wrote a Letter to Clarity and My Career Wrote Me Back

> "As is a tale, so is life: not how long it is,
> but how good it is, is what matters."
>
> —Seneca

It's nearly time to close this book out, but first let's look back at its most salient lessons.

First and foremost, doing work you care about and doing work that matters is not reserved for a select and special few. Career satisfaction is not a limited resource. It therefore doesn't have to be something you dream about and yet don't experience.

Clarity doesn't magically happen to us. The clouds don't miraculously part solely because we say that's what we want. We have to *act* to get the clarity we seek. We have to do the inner work *and* the outer work. When we do that, the results will feel pretty close to magic.

Reinventing your career is about committing to overcoming obstacles that seem insurmountable, being scared and taking the risk anyway, and being willing to accept the consequences if it doesn't go exactly as planned. It's about being hell bent on not giving up. It's about actually *doing* the work you think you can't do . . . no matter where, no matter what.

How you spend your days is one of the most important decisions you make, and you are asked to make this decision every single day. No matter what you are doing today, if you hate it you don't have to do it again tomorrow. You don't have to settle for a lifetime of doing work you hate. You don't have to sit back and waste your talents. You don't have to watch others live lives of sig-nificance, influence, passion, and success while you sit back and dream. Those can be the reality of your career, too.

Writing letters to something (or someone) that is showing up in your life and creating a challenge for you—your fear, your frustration, your desire, your confusion, your mean boss, your dream job, and so on—is the epitome of practicality and hope. Writing allows you to distance yourself from your worries and to get clear, invite something or someone into a conversation with you—in private—and act it all out in the safety of words. It helps you see how real a dream or a wish could be.

Writing letters is a two-dimensional experience that allows you to risk just enough to pretend that what you want is already happening or what you need to do is already being done. What feels crazy and impossible in your head becomes exciting and possible once it's down on paper. The real value in writing the letters is that you realize that you have it in you to turn your ideas and dreams into reality once you write them down. Show up in the writing *every* time by being specific and honest about what you want—the answers will be there if you do.

Without receiving permission from yourself, stepping into the work you want to do will prove nearly impossible. Hand yourself the permission slip you require—no expiration date and no restrictions. You don't have to bow to another authority.

Some people believe it's best to live with no regrets. I disagree, because to do so would be to miss out on valuable information, new insight, countering points of view, and new ways of looking at old facts. The *"If only this, then that"* kind of thinking is actually good for you. At least it can be, if you use it to your advantage rather than marinating in it to the point where you feel you lack control of your life.

Align your work with your highest values. No matter what.

Your greatness comes at the intersection of interest, aptitude, practice, com-mitment, and belief. No matter how much you love doing a certain activity, how much you practice, how good you are and how committed you are, you'll never achieve greatness if you don't believe you're already great enough to achieve it. It's not always easy however to access your greatness when you're struggling to find your way. When you're in that place, borrow the belief that others have in you to keep going until you can tap into it yourself. Use your support network. You have the gifts of "your why", your desire to make a contribution, your inspiration to make a difference, your ability to do whatever you can imagine in your mind, and your default to succeed. You must use them.

You can't do this alone. Nobody who ever reached true greatness at anything ever has or ever will. There's nothing like knowing someone is rooting for you and they have your back when your drive starts to slow. Find a mentor, a coach, a community, and share your goals with them. Then, let them support and help you the best way they know how.

Complacency is the enemy of change and the most significant barrier to career reinvention. Find a way to create urgency when it comes to your career and then maintain it so you can drop out of the Cycle of Complacency and drop into your crazy good work.

You will not discover your passion by reading a book or taking a test. Passion can't be found from a list on a page or by setting an intention and taking zero actions to generate results. You'll discover it by acting on a desire and on the nudges you are getting, putting yourself in situations where possibilities will present themselves to you and then getting good at that thing you've pursued. As the famous educational reformer John Dewey wrote, "You need to catch interest before you can hold on to it."[1]

Surprises make life interesting. If you search for a life that has no tension, one that is scripted and obvious and safe, then little in it will be satisfying. Experiments can remind you that you are in the game and you get to call the shots. Experiments also keep you out of rehearsal mode, which happens when you research, analyze, and plan at the exclusion of doing. It's fine to rehearse and get yourself ready, but the real information you need comes when you take the stage on opening night. With each experiment you do, you become clearer on your priorities, you answer questions you didn't even know you had, and the momentum you create from each experiment will lead to even more action, as you make your way toward the career path that is new and exciting and interesting to you. In addition, when you experiment you give the real world a chance to test your ideas, which it will do far more thoroughly than your imagination ever could.

The way we learn about ourselves is by doing and then observing how we react to what crosses our path. The moment you say yes to acting on the desire you have for a certain career path you invite the possibility for passion to come in. That is one of the best gifts you can ever give yourself. Passion needs room to flow, and by experimenting and committing to a type of work "as if" it were your new career, you give passion a place to land. The goal with the experiments is to first create momentum and then get information you can use to inform your next steps.

Fear is information about a *feeling*. It's not information about a *reality*. When you are up against a fear, the first question you must ask yourself is, "Am I okay?" If the answer is yes, move on to the next question, which is, "Is what I want more important than the fear?" If the answer is yes, keep going.

If the answer is no, it's time to go back and determine your true desire.

Finally, if you find yourself stuck in a holding pattern, use the following question to help get you out: "What if (insert fear) were no longer important to me?" Focusing on the answer to that will usually help you blow through the barriers that keep taking you out of the game.

One of the best ways to find your voice is to create a new movement that you can get behind, so that whenever the voice inside of you starts ranting on about why you should be choosing a career that is "practical" and "possible," rather than one that seems "crazy" and "unreasonable," you will be strong in your response. Identify your guiding principles and allow them to light your way.

Your voice is one of the most powerful gifts you have. Own it, share it, and use it every chance you get. If you want to get clarity on your career, your voice needs to be strong and unencumbered, and you have to be willing to put yourself, your ideas, and your beliefs out there in a big and bold way.

There is an art to reinventing your career that goes beyond trying to figure out the work you want to do and how you want to do it. It starts with play and ends with giving. In Chapter 10, I offered eleven recommendations for how to do that. So, are you ready?

Key Points

If I were forced to turn this book into one page, here are the lessons I would want to make sure you had discovered, remembered or re-imagined.

- When it comes to doing work you care about, don't wait around for someone else to crown you worthy. Give yourself permission and jump.

- Writing it down makes a difference. Write your letters, act on behalf of what you wrote, and then let the Universe and everyone in your life conspire in your favor to help make what you want to happen, happen.

- You get to do work you love and care about. Period.

- When you have the support and love of other people, you are more powerful than you could ever be on your own. Ask for help, be specific, and allow the resources to show up.

- The most essential lesson of this whole book: If you truly want to switch your career, hurry up and show it.

And remember this . . .

"I'm Not Sure What Will Happen . . . I Just Know Something Will"

At my CrossFit gym there's a saying, "This shit really works." By "shit" we mean going all out, getting our butts in the gym every day, and eating strictly the Paleo way, which means consuming no dairy, no grains, no sugar, no corn, no legumes, limited fruit and eating primarily grass fed and grass finished lean meats and a variety of low starch vegetables. If you do that, the regimen works. You get crazy strong. You feel good inside. You sleep better, get sick less often, and look better than you ever have. And you can take on nearly any physical challenge that presents itself, which comes in handy far more than you would think.

Before I started doing CrossFit, I was the queen of long, slow distance training. I spent decades running umpteen miles a week, doing weights in the gym, eating no fat and no meat, counting calories, and following conventional wisdom. I had no idea how rapidly doing CrossFit would turn every belief I had about fitness and nutrition on its head. I had no idea what would happen when I completely changed how I "did" food and fitness. I just knew something would happen . . . and it did.

It's not easy to behave differently or to commit to making a change when an outcome is unknown. It's not easy to give up old patterns and behaviors and hope the new ones will pan out. However, that's exactly what you need to do to achieve your greatness, to live your finest hour, to do the work that is in your heart. When you give up everything and put every last bit of strength and effort into doing that thing you dream of doing and it seems too big, reflect back to every other goal you've ever committed to accomplishing in your life. Whether it was completing a race, getting your first job, losing weight, writing a book, moving to a new city, or even cleaning your house, something happened as a result of taking action on behalf of your commitment.

It's possible that what happened wasn't what you thought was going to happen or what you wanted to happen, and it's possible that what happened may have been better than anything you could have imagined, but something *always* happened. Maybe when you committed to making a change all that happened was that you proved to yourself that it was not the direction for you. That's still *something happening.*

The thing is, even though all of us know on some level that something is going to happen if we simply take action, we still get taken out by thoughts like these:

- "What if I do such and such and nothing happens?"
- "I'd like to try it, but what will happen?"
- "It's too risky. What if nothing comes of it?"

These are the kinds of questions that stop people from starting that business, from switching careers, from putting their hearts on the line, from taking the first running step, from taking a chance.

It's not easy to go to a place where you are not able to predict with any degree of certainty what it will all end up looking like 365 days from now. But this year is going to go by whether or not you commit to changing your situation. You can know for sure that if you continue to do the same old thing when it comes to your career then the same old thing is going to be the result. I suspect that if you've read this far this idea sounds profoundly uninteresting to you, therefore, what other choice do you have than to commit and *do* no matter what, no matter how uneasy and uncertain you feel, no matter how difficult the task, and no matter how many times your quiet inner voice or loud inner critic tries to put you back in your comfortable place.

When you start to wander off track, review the simple mantra "I'm not sure what will happen, but I know something will" . . . and then go do your crazy good work.

WRITE THAT SH*T DOWN!

It's almost time for you to begin a new chapter in your career reinvention process but before you go, you have two final writing exercises.

Priming the Pump

In this final "priming the pump exercise" I have only two questions for you.

1. Who is the person you want to become?
2. How will you measure your life when it's time to look back?

Write a Letter to Clarity

I hope that by now you have reached a new level of clarity about what's next for you. For this final exercise, write a letter to Clarity and tell it exactly what you've learned about what you need, what you want, and what you're looking forward to as you take your next steps.

After writing this letter, one of my clients told me, *"Up until this point I still had a lot of ideas and was worried I wouldn't be able to pick just one to pursue. But when I wrote this letter it became so obvious what I should do that I can't believe I hadn't seen it. It was like I finally showed up and when I did that, my career did, too."*

I had a similar experience when I wrote to Clarity, but unlike my client, the first time I wrote to Clarity I did it at the beginning of my career reinvention process, rather than at the end. In fact, it was one of the first letters I ever wrote. At the time I thought that if I wanted to get clarity I'd better start there. The problem was that I wanted the end result of the entire process you've just been through without having to do the work.

My first letter reveals someone who was scattered, frustrated, and desperate. When I came back to do another letter to Clarity at the end of my letter-writing process, the experience was much different. Similar to my client, I felt like I had come home. Finally, I had knocked on the door and my career said, "C'mon in. I've been expecting you."

Notes

Introduction

1. *American Time Use Survey*, United States Bureau of Labor Statistics, 2007. Website: BLS.gov.
2. Henriette Anne Klauser, *Write It Down, Make It Happen* (New York, Scribner, 2000): p. 34.
3. In exchange for using their case studies as part of this book, especially when they involve sections of their own journals and letters, I agreed to change the name and specific, identifying details to protect each person's privacy.

Chapter 2   I Wrote a Letter to Regret and Opportunity Wrote Me Back

1. Neale J. Roese, Ph.D., *If Only: How to Turn Regret into Opportunity* (New York: Broadway Books, 2005), Kindle edition.

Chapter 5   I Wrote a Letter to My Greatness and It Told Me to Get My Butt in Gear

1. Malcolm Gladwell, *Outliers: The Story of Success* (New York: Little, Brown and Company, 2008): p. 41.
2. Johnson O'Connor Research Foundation, http://www.jocrf.org.
3. Geoffrey Colvin, *Talent Is Overrated: What Really Separates World Class Performers from Everybody Else* (New York: Portfolio Trade, 2010), Kindle edition.

4. A letter from Benjamin Franklin's father to his son, as cited by Colvin: Location: 1730-36, Kindle edition.

5. Nathan Milstein, as cited by Anders K. Ericcson, Michael J. Prietula, and Edward T. Cokely, "The Making of An Expert," *Harvard Business Review* (July 2007): p. 71.

6. Anders K. Ericsson, Ralf T. Krampe, and Clemens Tesch-Römer, "The Role of Deliberate Practice in the Acquisition of Expert Performance," *Psychological Review,* vol. 100, issue 3 (July 1993): pp. 363–406.

7. Benjamin S. Bloom, *Developing Talent in Young People* (New York: Ballantine Books, 1985).

Chapter 7   I Wrote a Letter to Desire and Passion Wrote Me Back

1. From a personal interview with Ashley Murray that took place on July 14, 2012.

2. John Dewey, as cited by Todd Kashdan, *Curious? Discover the Missing Ingredient to a Fulfilling Life.* (New York: William Morrow, 2009): p. 73.

3. Julien Smith, *The Flinch.* (The Domino Project, 2011), Kindle edition (Chapter: The Flinch; Section: Your World as a Corridor, paragraph 10).

4. Seth Godin, *The Dip: A Little Book that Teaches You When to Quit.* (New York: Portfolio, 2007), Kindle edition (Section: I Feel Like Giving Up, paragraph 6).

5. Ibid: Kindle edition.

Chapter 10   I Wrote a Letter to Reinven-
tion and My Mojo Wrote Me Back

1. Michael Murphy and, Rhea A. White, *The Psychic Side of Sports.* (City, Longman Higher Education, 1979).

Chapter 11   I Wrote a Letter to Clarity and
My Career Wrote Me Back

1. John Dewey, as cited by Todd Kashdan, *Curious? Discover the Missing Ingredient to a Fulfilling Life* (New York: William Morrow, 2009): p. 73.

Appendix

More Letters

If the sixteen letters in *Career Switch* have helped you get clarity on what you want to do and you're really itching to write some more, then you're in luck. There are materials on my website, created especially for you, which will give you more ideas for letters you can write yourself while on your career switch journey. So, get out your magic pen and head over to Career-Switch.org/bonus-letters.

Writing

If you're looking for a great, fast, and reliable writer for your blog or magazine, I'm a freelance writer specializing in career and personal development topics. I'd love to write for you. You can find out why you might want to hire me at HotButtonCopy.com.

Articles and More

Look, there's more! If you've read this far, I hope you found the experience valuable. If you would like more, head on over to CareerSwitch.org, where you'll find a community of other readers who are hell bent on living a life of significance by doing work that lights them up.

You will find a number of writing exercises, letter ideas, and more, that did not make it into the final version of this book, including:

- Interviews from people who have reinvented their careers in big ways.
- A Career Hacker Unplugged series where I interview entrepreneurs and work-life passionaistas on how to do the work you love.

- And much more! All of the information and resources are free and you don't need to register to receive them.

If you enjoyed the book, or even if you didn't, I'd love to get your feedback. Reviews on Amazon are greatly appreciated but if you would rather just email me directly, please feel free to do so directly from CareerSwitch.org.

Share the Love

Did you find that writing the letters has been helpful in your career reinvention process? I think writing down your ideas, thoughts and dreams is the epitome of practicality and hope. It's optimistic and gives you the space to unload and then reboot so you can tackle anything you want.

If you agree, feel free to spread the good word on Twitter with this tweet: *Check out Career Switch by @melaniward. Valuable read if you're hell bent on doing work you care about – www.careerswitch.org.*

Gratitude

I have relished the idea of writing this section. I want to call out every last person who made this possible and helped me see my way through when I lacked the clarity to do so myself. Just as nothing is possible without the support of others, accomplishing something you've held in your heart for so long means nothing if you can't share that joy with those who helped make it happen.

The first thanks go to my family. Mom, you have always been my greatest cheerleader and the one who encouraged me to find the joy in life first. Dad, your work ethic always inspires me and I'm grateful that no matter how many times I swayed and went off course you never doubted me for a second. Topo, my bother, thank you for sticking with me and supporting me, in more ways than one, throughout all of the crazy turns I've made. All of you have supported me in every possible way and I owe everything I am to you.

To Chris, my husband, who has spent the past seven years listening to every harebrained idea I've had and stayed with me anyway. Thank you for saying, "We'll make it happen," and then making sure we do. And to my daughter Dylan who was always there to remind me that words on a page don't hold a candle to a spontaneous dance party. You are the best!

To Sandy Grason, my BFF, confidante, and partner in crime. This book never would have been written if it weren't for you telling me to: "Just go write. Do your work." For all of the afternoon movies, marathon conversations on the couch, and countless texts to say, "Dude, are you writing?" thank you. Thanks for always being my person. We will retreat together again some day.

To Stephanie Gunning, my editor, who stuck with me for three years and finally called me out on my BS to get this book done. I would still be mapping out the idea and bothering people with my dream if it weren't for you. Thank you for making me a better writer and for making me love the craft even more.

To Debbie Ally, Julie Smith, Andrea Vahl, Tara Powers, Cynthia Stadd, Melissa Jones, and Sandy Grason (again) for "shazam-ing" me that night at The Med. It really worked! I can't imagine what my life would be like without your laughter, love, and support. I love you all.

To Jennifer Louden, one of the people I admire most in the world. I will never forget that afternoon in Taos when you looked at me and said, "Melani, you *are* a writer." Thank you for believing in me long before I was able to get on board.

To all of my clients and others mentioned in this book for teaching me through your stories and allowing me to glimpse into your lives. You helped me bring many of my ideas to life and for that I am truly grateful.

To Hillary Harris who I spent nearly every afternoon with while writing this book. Being able to chill out, laugh about our kids, talk about WOD's and eat brisket without worrying about word counts and deadlines was a gift. Here's to many more nights in the 'hood.

To my mother-in-law, Nancy, who said, "I'm challenging you to write the book you've been talking about." I needed that. Thanks for not letting me get away with putting it off any more.

To my uncle Meatball, who passed away from ALS, my uncle Eddie, who passed away from pulmonary fibrosis, and my aunts, Patsy and Chase, who are alive and well. Thank you for your love and for being constant sources of inspiration. You are phenomenal people and I feel lucky beyond words to call you my family.

Finally, to my sister Shelly who died when we were young. You are the butterfly of my life, my guardian angel, and not a day goes by that I don't miss you. This is for you.

About Melani

Melani Ward is a former history teacher, counselor, and athletic coach turned serial career hopper. These days she works as a copywriter, content creator, and career switch enthusiast. She spent the first twenty years of her career hell bent on doing work she cares about and now hopes to help others do the same. She holds graduate degrees in counselor education and sociology, and when not writing, she enjoys playing with her husband, daughter, and dog on the playground that is Boulder, Colorado